44 0561384 X

 **University of
Hertfordshire**

Learning and Information Services

Hatfield Campus Learning Resources Centre
College Lane Hatfield Herts AL10 9AB
Renewals: Tel 01707 284673 Mon-Fri 12 noon-8pm only

This book is in heavy demand and is due back strictly by the last
date stamped below. A fine will be charged for the late return of
items.

ONE WEEK LOAN

D1428405

ABOUT THE AUTHOR

Lenore Wadsworth Hervey, Ph.D., ADTR, NCC, REAT, is a senior associate faculty member in the Dance/Movement Therapy and Counseling Psychology Programs at Antioch New England Graduate School, Keene, NH. She received her doctoral degree from The Union Institute in the fields of Creativity Studies and Research Methodologies. She is currently chair of the Research Subcommittee of the American Dance Therapy Association.

After performing and teaching dance professionally, she began her career as a dance/movement therapist. Her clinical experiences in addictions and gerontology contributed to her present commitment to a spiritual approach in dance/movement therapy. She is similarly committed to maintaining the artistic essence of the creative arts therapies. In addition to teaching, her current work includes a private supervision practice in dance/movement and expressive arts therapies, and consultation in individual and collaborative creativity.

ARTISTIC INQUIRY
IN
DANCE/MOVEMENT
THERAPY
Creative Research Alternatives

By

LENORE WADSWORTH HERVEY

With a Foreword by Shaun McNiff

Charles C Thomas
PUBLISHER • LTD.
·SPRINGFIELD · ILLINOIS · U.S.A.·

Published and Distributed Throughout the World by

CHARLES C THOMAS • PUBLISHER, LTD.
2600 South First Street
Springfield, Illinois 62704

This book is protected by copyright. No part of
it may be reproduced in any manner without
written permission from the publisher.

© 2000 by CHARLES C THOMAS • PUBLISHER, LTD.

ISBN 0-398-07108-X (hard)
ISBN 0-398-07109-8 (paper)

Library of Congress Catalog Card Number: 00-042305

With THOMAS BOOKS *careful attention is given to all details of manufacturing and design.
It is the Publisher's desire to present books that are satisfactory as to their physical qualities and
artistic possibilities and appropriate for their particular use.* THOMAS BOOKS *will be true
to those laws of quality that assure a good name and good will.*

Printed in the United States of America
RR-R-3

Library of Congress Cataloging-in-Publication Data

Hervey, Lenore Wadsworth.
    Artistic inquiry in dance/movement therapy: creative research alternatives/by Lenore
Wadsworth Hervey; with a foreword by Shaun McNiff.
    p. cm.
    Includes bibliographical references and index.
    ISBN 0-398-07108-X – ISBN 0-398-07109-8 (pbk.)
    1. Dance therapy. 2. Movement therapy. 3. Arts–Psychology. I. Title.

RC489.D3 H47 2000
615.8'5155–dc21

00-042305

This work is dedicated to:

my father for his focused devotion to his work,

my family for their patience with me,

and my students for being such outstanding teachers.

UNIVERSITY OF HERTFORDSHIRE
HATFIELD CAMPUS LRC
HATFIELD AL10 9AD   350389

BIB	0-398-07109-8
CLASS	615.85155 HER
LOCATION	owl
BARCODE	44 0561384 x

FOREWORD

The creative arts therapies have a unique and even enviable potential to transform the pursuit of knowledge. We are a richly interdisciplinary field combining the resources of the arts, science, healing, and service to others. The creative arts therapies have also demonstrated an adventurous pragmatism in creating partnerships with mental health, education, medicine and various human service professions. As a professional community united by a belief in the healing powers of the arts, we have been open to collaborations with diverse institutions ranging from traditional therapeutic settings to the corporate world.

The greatest obstacle to fully realizing this potential is the adjunctive identity that has characterized the profession since its inception. Although many pioneers and practitioners have made successful efforts to affirm the primary therapeutic features of the different creative arts therapies, there has been a particularly strong tendency to rely on behavioral science paradigms whenever discussing the subject of research. These attitudes and practices have kept us on the periphery in relation to research focused on the creation of new knowledge.

A lack of appreciation by the outside world and other professional groups can be approached as a concrete and very fixable problem. When others do not understand what we do and how it can be of use to the world, we are given a clear platform to present what we can offer. I have discovered that academic and professional communities as well as the general public, are fascinated by the integration of the arts, therapy, healing, and psychological understanding. There are great opportunities yet to be realized by the creative arts therapies and perhaps the most challenging obstacle our profession faces its own self-image.

In accepting the argument that we need to justify what we do through "accepted" behavioral and social science research methods, we have placed ourselves under the dominion of concepts and methods that do not resonate with what we are, what we do, and what we need to know in order to improve ourselves and more effectively communicate with the world. We have lost valuable time and resources in attempting to adapt to the research paradigms of other disciplines, that now openly acknowledge how the restrictions of their "conceptual blueprints in comparison with the complexities of empirical phenomena" make it difficult to open to the unexpected (Portes, 2000, p. 4).

In *Art-Based Research* (1998) I describe how artistic inquiry might even have something to offer the larger scientific community in understanding experience. Many of the world's great scientists have been intrigued by connections with the arts, realizing that the creative imagination integrates analytic and aesthetic ways of knowing. The pragmatic and open-minded researcher realizes that it is the unpredictable discoveries, often stimulated by factors outside the lines of conventional inquiry, that move science forward in significant ways. The creative imagination functions best when it is free to make new connections amongst the most varied mix of ingredients.

Doctoral study by creative arts therapists within settings like The Union Institute and the emerging European Graduate School in Switzerland is a great frontier for our profession. Although there are many benefits to researching the creative arts therapies within social and behavioral science doctoral programs there are unavoidable issues of having to accommodate to the research methods of other disciplines which become the dominant partner. We need to create communities of scholars committed to supporting and inspiring one another in the creation a new research tradition based upon artistic inquiry.

The older and more accepted methods of research used by other disciplines can teach us a great deal about disciplined inquiry, the criticism of knowledge, and the creation of new knowledge. My own doctoral research in the psychology of art used relatively standard behavioral science methods to investigate the subject of artistic motivation. My faculty advisor saw that although I was mastering certain psychological research methods, my art was not involved. He encouraged me to expand the inquiry by making and exhibiting my own paintings.

At that time in the mid-1970s my psychological and artistic investigations happened on parallel tracks. Although there was certainly an integration of some kind taking place in my work, the two modes of inquiry stayed within the lines of their respective spheres. It never occurred to me that my art-making could be used as a valid method of inquiry.

Later work as a supervisor of graduate students in creative arts therapy resulted in my paradigm shift. I realized how the therapeutic methods that students loved and wanted to master, were not being used as modes of inquiry in their thesis research. The needs of students to use their own creative expression as a way of understanding the healing powers of art was my impetus in exploring new ways of approaching research (McNiff, 1998).

It is time to establish a more universal research tradition that respects the inherent intelligence of the arts. "Art is a way of knowing" as Pat Allen (1995) writes and perhaps our most ancient mode of pondering and coming to terms with the problems, contradictions, and powers of human experience. But as Stephen Levine notes, not all art-making is research (2000, p. 3). What are the differences? What type of artistic inquiry will contribute to the creation of a useful and intelligent research tradition? What should we avoid? How do we connect artistic inquiry with discursive and analytic language (Levine, p. 3)? These issues and challenges emerging from the creation of a new art-based research tradition are fascinating, not only in terms of the field of creative arts therapy, but within the broader domain of epistemology and disciplined inquiry into human experience.

The most formidable problem faced by creative arts therapy in exploring these opportunities is the belief commonly held by our educational programs, professional associations, and professional certification authorities that we have to justify ourselves through conceptual frameworks and research methods that do not emerge directly from our practice. This is a strange and unique dilemma that some feel betrays an attitude of inferiority. My sense is that these identity issues have evolved from the early advantages creative arts therapists experienced by attaching themselves to what were then the more mainstream and acceptable methods of the behavioral and social sciences. Although we have now outgrown this need to empower ourselves by relying on others, the adjustment to autonomy is not easy. There is a need for strong, intelligent, confident, and clear voices to guide the formation of a new tradition.

It is within this larger context of opportunities that Lenore Wadsworth Hervey's book, *Artistic Inquiry in Dance/Movement Therapy*, is being published. This is a clear and engaging text that provides an overview of how artistic inquiry relates to the larger world of research. With great respect for other traditions, Wadsworth Hervey articulates the unique and unrealized potential of the arts as ways of exploring the world while also providing a structure and introduction to ideas and methods that will guide researchers. I especially appreciate how the author makes useful and intelligent links to philosophy and the history of ideas, something that is profoundly absent in psychology. The breadth of this analysis will make this book illuminating to researchers in any field.

Attitudes toward research in the creative arts therapies have generally viewed the arts as data that are examined through behavioral science research methods. I appreciate the way Wadsworth Hervey clearly distinguishes this analysis of art materials from art making as a method of inquiry. She supports my long-standing belief that art-based research does not necessarily fit inside the parameters of the quantitative-qualitative dichotomy of behavioral science. Artistic inquiry is not yet another of the many types to be listed under qualitative research methods. Although I respect what qualitative behavioral science researchers do, art can be something quite different. Art-based research might often relate to behavioral science but we are not contained by it. The phenomena of the arts must be allowed to speak for themselves within their unique environments.

This expansion of possibilities recognizes that behavioral science research methods may be the best vehicles for examining certain types of issues in the creative arts therapies. Lenore Wadsworth Hervey and I simply encourage the "addition" of artistic inquiry to the range of options. We are not making a one-sided insistence that a particular way of doing research is the best way to approach every situation.

In addition to making important contributions to furthering inquiry in all artistic media, Wadsworth Hervey focuses on particular dynamics of research within dance and movement. I have a special interest in kinesis and flow as a basic condition of human experience. Everything I do within life and the arts is grounded on a sensitivity to the process and mystery of movements constantly emerging from another. As we know from the ancient Greece of Heraclitus, the foundational principles of Buddhism, and contemporary physics, nature and consciousness are in a state of constant flux. Movement is the basic principle of existence and we know so little about it. We have yet to seriously reflect upon Ahab's question in *Moby Dick*, " Is Ahab, Ahab? Is it I, God, or who, that lifts this arm?"

Where creative arts therapies have adapted themselves to the very linear scientific paradigms of behavioral science, I have argued that we should look more closely at links to physics. The physicist David Bohm describes how "thought itself is in an actual process of movement" that is connected to the larger "flow in the movement of matter in general" (1980, p. ix). Bohm used his bodily experience as a way of understanding problems in advanced physics. Like Einstein, he trusted his intuitive physical sensations as a way of grasping the complex movements of phenomena. This laboratory of personal experience enabled Bohm to penetrate depths that were not accessible by logical and mathematical analysis.

So rather than thinking about movement from the window of cognition, we can invert the relationship and know more about thought by approaching it via movement. Can you imagine a research center operating in a dance studio where investigators move freely and reflect upon the flow of their gestures; the feelings they have before, during, and after the sessions; the effects of the environment on their movements; the ways in which other people in the room influence them; moving in silence vs. moving with a drum; the way in which movements emerge naturally from one another during an improvisation; the use of movements to understand and re-frame our psychological problems and conflicts, and even the use of bodily sensations and movement interactions with others to re-vision how we relate to one another in the workplace?

Rather than utilizing psychology to "explain" movement, imagine moving to gain a better understanding of psychological well-being. If the most advanced physicists of the past century respected these methods of inquiry, why can't the creative arts therapies?

Faced with these exciting opportunities that are affirmed by advances in science, dance/movement therapy together with the other creative arts therapies continue to operate almost exclusively with the boxes of the most conventional behavioral science research methods. Wadsworth Hervey documents how researchers in dance/movement therapy have given no attention to artistic inquiry and she reports the absence of any dialogue about art-based research in her profession's publications. She presents the work of Bill T. Jones in creating the multimedia performance *Still/Here* as an example of an extended work of artistic inquiry that can stimulate researchers in her discipline to dance in a more open and creative space.

Artistic Inquiry in Dance/Movement Therapy will augment the practice of research in dance/movement therapy where there is sometimes a tendency to overcompensate for the body-oriented nature of the work with a belief that the discipline is not conceptual enough. As dance/movement therapy re-discovers the intelligence of the body and nature's movements, it will achieve a more complete integration with the mind. In addition to serving her discipline of dance/movement therapy, Lenore Wadsworth Hervey crosses over to the larger context of creative research and reminds us all to stay rooted in the immediate physical experiences that inform everything. Movement is our common source and let's use its wisdom and creativity to gain a more complete understanding of ourselves and the world.

Shaun McNiff

REFERENCES

Allen, P. (1995). *Art is a way of knowing.* Boston: Shambhala.

Bohm, D. (1980). *Wholeness and the implicate order.* London: Routledge and Kegan Paul.

Levine, S. (2000). Research in the expressive arts: A poetic way of knowing. *EGS (European Graduate School) News, 3-4.*

McNiff, S. (1998). *Art-based research.* London, Jessica Kingsley.

Portes, A. (2000). The hidden abode: Sociology as analysis of the unexpected. *American Sociological Review,* Vol. 65, 1-18.

PREFACE

This book offers a compelling research alternative for dance/movement (and other creative arts) therapists who recognize how valuable artistic ways of knowing are to the theory and practice of their profession. It encourages participation in a mode of inquiry that invites fully authentic engagement, inspires excitement about discovery, and builds confidence in abilities to contribute to the professional body of research literature. Artistic inquiry requires the combination of creative, artistic, and aesthetic skills used in service of the embodied therapeutic relationship that qualiffies dance/movement therapists as unique researchers.

Artistic inquiry is defined as research that: (1) uses artistic methods of gathering, analyzing, and/or presenting data; (2) engages in and acknowledges a creative process, and (3) is motivated and determined by the aesthetic values of the researcher(s). These three defining characteristics are theoretically and practically examined in depth and accompanied by examples of artistic inquiry relevant to dance/movement therapy. Interdisciplinary support for the validity of artistic inquiry is drawn from a rich field of resources, including philosophy, social sciences, education, and the arts. *Still/Here*, a multimedia dance work by Bill T. Jones, is presented as a work of art that can be viewed as artistic inquiry. Jones' use of dance as the primary expressive medium, drawing from the verbal and non-verbal narratives of people living with terminal illnesses, exemplifies the potential that artistic inquiry has for dance/movement therapy.

The book concludes with recommendations for the promotion and evaluation of artistic inquiry projects. Throughout, it upholds a vision of research as a vital, satisfying, and essential part of a dance/movement therapist's career.

L.W.H.

CONTENTS

ARTISTIC INQUIRY
IN
DANCE/MOVEMENT THERAPY

Chapter 1

INTRODUCTION

ARTISTIC INQUIRY CAME to my attention through the writings of Shaun McNiff and Elliot Eisner, who have for many years been devoted to the promotion of alternative forms of research within their respective fields of creative arts therapy and education. With admiration for their work, I attempt here to further develop the idea of artistic inquiry through clear definition and through identification of contemporary research that fits this definition. I hope to promote artistic inquiry as a form of research compatible with the values and unique skills of dance/movement therapists, thereby offering it as a useful tool in support of the profession's growth.

Following this introductory chapter, literature that discusses the recent development of artistic inquiry (called arts-based research by some) will be reviewed, with special attention to Eisner's and McNiff's contributions. The scholarly context for this project will be an interdisciplinary field that crosses education, the social sciences, and a small subsection of psychology that includes the creative arts therapies. This scope is determined by my inquiry's purpose and by these fields' recognition of artistic methods of research.

Artistic inquiry's potential for dance/movement therapy will be explored in four chapters: one for each of artistic inquiry's three major descriptors, and the fourth describes a dance work that exemplifies all three. Throughout, illustrative references will be made to a small research project entitled "Identifying dance/movement therapy students' feelings and attitudes about doing research" which is described in its entirety in the Appendix. The concluding chapter will examine the applicability of artistic inquiry to research in dance/movement therapy and will consider methods of assessing the quality and value of projects using artistic inquiry.

The following pages of this chapter introduce the research problem and the methods used to investigate it. Five terms essential to this discussion (artistic inquiry, research, creative arts therapy, dance/movement therapy, and science) are defined for use in this context. The idea of truth is then explored to a greater extent, as I see its meaning and relevance at this time as controversial in the field of research. The chapter then moves this investigation beyond concerns with truth and concludes with a discussion of two concepts deeply relevant to artistic inquiry: aesthetics and authenticity.

THE RESEARCH PROBLEM

> I believe that the greatest research asset of the creative arts therapies profession is the fact that we cannot be exclusively identified with either art or science. (McNiff, 1986, p. 281)

In the topography of disciplines, dance/movement therapy, like all the creative arts therapies, is indeed located insecurely yet undeniably between the arts and what some would consider the science of psychology. This position creates some conflicts within and around the profession, one of which arises in efforts to produce and promote research in the field. Some well-meaning advisors to the field (Chaiklin, 1968, 1997; Holtz, 1990; Milberg, 1977) have strongly suggested that quantitative evidence of our clinical outcomes would garner recognition from administrators, insurance companies, and other power wielders in the mental healthcare system. Yet high quality research of this type, demonstrating the efficacy of any of the creative arts therapies, is still rarely evident in professional journals (Chaiklin, 1997; Edwards, 1993). As recently as 1996, Ritter and Low published a meta-analysis of research in dance/movement therapy that indicated a body of literature "rife with methodological problems" (p. 258) that could not strongly support the therapeutic successes it seemed to suggest.

McNiff (1993), Landy (1993), Junge and Linesch (1993), Knill, Barba and Fuchs (1995), and other creative arts therapists have recently offered alternatives to quantitative studies, but potential researchers seem to be slow to understand or appreciate their value. Many still believe that hope lies exclusively in striving for recognition within the human sciences, and so have turned away from the unique skills and strengths of their arts.

This dilemma extends beyond dance/movement and the other creative arts therapies. Much of the modern world has been convinced that the scientific method is the only way to authoritative knowledge and truth, and only recently, in the postmodern era, have larger numbers of people begun to question this paradigm and its power. Yet many dance/movement therapists are still unaware that there are valid research options beyond the positivist, quantitative approach. Now, as postmodern proponents of qualitative methods in many fields are challenging traditional and modern understandings of inquiry, dance/movement therapists could truly have the "freedom of inquiry" that McNiff offered in 1986. In this discussion, I, like McNiff in the following passage, extend the call for alternative methods of research beyond even the qualitative, and into the realm of the artistic.

> We must . . . become involved in questioning the nature of research in order to protect and advance the artistic interests of our profession. We cannot rely on the larger behavioral science community to articulate our scholarly priorities. (1986, p. 279)

I have become involved in this question over the past ten years while teaching research to dance/movement therapy students. I feel compelled to respond to my student's desires to participate in modes of inquiry that will invite their full authentic engagement, inspire their excitement about what they could discover, and build confidence in their ability to contribute to their profession through research. Unfortunately, traditional forms of research estrange too many from the pursuit of knowledge and leave them feeling hopeless about its usefulness for their professional futures. As a dance/movement and expressive arts therapist myself, as well as an educator, I have had my own encounter with traditional research methods that has contributed to my understanding of theirs. This project is very much motivated by a commitment to my students and an equal commitment to the art form of dance as vital to every aspect of the authentic practice of dance/movement therapy.

METHODS

The method of this inquiry began with a deep and prolonged exposure to the attitudes of dance/movement therapy students toward research, during which I came to know their struggles and their learning styles intimately. As part of teaching and the necessary ongoing learning about research, I had been reading professional publications such as the *American Journal of Dance Therapy* and *The Arts in Psychotherapy* regularly. I noted the nature and quality of the research in dance/movement and other creative arts therapies, as compared to that presented in the psychological and educational journals. In 1995, the interdisciplinary journal called *Qualitative Inquiry* published its first volume, and my concept of what research could be exploded beyond all previous boundaries. Although I had been familiar with qualitative methods, as well the idea of artistic inquiry through McNiff, the articles in this journal consistently challenged previous limitations of method and imagination. I attended the 1996 Association of Educational Research Conference on Qualitative Research entitled "Improvisations and Deep Structures: Alternative Forms of Data Representation," where I had the opportunity to see several examples of research presented in artistic forms, most notably dramatic.

My search continued with an extensive exploration of the literature about alternative forms of research, creative process, aesthetics, and the philosophy of the new sciences. I began to formulate my own understanding of what artistic inquiry could be and drafted a provisional definition. With this definition in mind, I presented the idea of artistic inquiry to my students and to colleagues at professional conferences, receiving feedback as to its meaning and relevance to them and making adjustments in response. My exploration of theoretical writing on the subject continued as I compared theory with research that exemplified these concepts. The definition gradually evolved into what it is in this document.

Upon discovering Bill Moyers' interview with performer/choreographer Bill T. Jones, I recognized that one of Jones' recent works, *Still/Here*, epitomized what I envisioned artistic inquiry to be. I entered into an in-depth study of Jones and this particular work through multiple primary and secondary resources, including live performances and lectures. This process further clarified and challenged the meaning of artistic inquiry. The final stage of this investigation into artistic inquiry has entailed questioning its value and applicability to dance/movement therapy and anticipating how to support and evaluate future artistic inquiry projects.

DISCUSSION OF TERMS

Obviously the entirety of this document is devoted to an explication of artistic inquiry, but before going much farther it seems appropriate to succinctly clarify what I mean by the term. In addition, because they are frequently referred to but not further defined in later discussions, my understanding and use of the terms research, creative arts therapy, dance/movement therapy, and science are included here. Three other core concepts: art, creativity and aesthetics will be addressed in greater depth in subsequent chapters.

ARTISTIC INQUIRY. I have developed a tripartite definition for artistic inquiry. The more completely any given research meets the three criteria or descriptors, the more clearly it can be identified as artistic inquiry. Each of these criteria will be discussed in depth in their own chapters, complete with examples of research that exemplify the application of the concept.

1. Artistic inquiry uses artistic methods of gathering, analyzing, and/or presenting data.
2. Artistic inquiry engages in and acknowledges a creative process.
3. Artistic inquiry is motivated and determined by the aesthetic values of the researcher(s).

RESEARCH. I assume that the primary purpose of any inquiry is a fuller, deeper, more accurate understanding of something that is important to the inquirer. How the drive toward understanding is satisfied determines whether the process is considered research. The Research Subcommittee of the American Dance Therapy Association supplied a definition of research that is inclusive enough to be a beginning place for the purposes of this inquiry: "The systematic investigation of a particular area of knowledge. A process that includes data gathering, data analysis, and drawing conclusions based on the data" (American Dance Therapy Association 1998).

One characteristic of research that is not explicit in the above definition is the formulation of a guiding research question that clarifies the focus of inquiry. The research question (not necessarily a hypothesis, which is not useful to all forms of research) is also essential to developing appropriate methodology. I believe this is true of artistic inquiry as well, and its presence or absence may in fact be a distinguishing characteristic between art and artistic inquiry.

In addition, ethical behavior, although not a defining criterion, has also come to be an indispensable consideration when conducting research. Ethical treatment of human subjects and ethical use of research results are dictated by the professional code of ethics of the association to which the researchers belong. In my opinion, artistic inquiry, like other forms of research, needs to be equally answerable to these guidelines, as well as those determined by the context within which the research is carried out. If the researcher does not belong to a professional association, then breaches in ethical behavior become more difficult to assess.

CREATIVE ARTS THERAPY. This umbrella term refers to the group of similar professions that make psychotherapeutic use of the arts as their primary modality. Music, dance, art, poetry, drama, and expressive arts (an intermodal practice) therapy all have professional associations that were founded in the later half of the twentieth century and share a coalition organization that works cooperatively in the best interests of all the creative arts associations. Core to the philosophies of all the creative arts therapies is the assumption that engagement in the artistic/creative process is healing in and of itself. The making and subsequent use of art (in any medium) by a patient to further emotional, physical, intellectual, and spiritual integration is facilitated through interventions made by an artist/therapist who is trained in counseling practices and psychological theory as well as his or her respective art field.

DANCE/MOVEMENT THERAPY. The American Dance Therapy Association defines dance/movement therapy as "the psychotherapeutic use of movement as a process which furthers the emotional, cognitive and physical integration of the individual" (American Dance Therapy Association, 1969).

In the mid-twentieth century, the field of dance/movement therapy was pioneered by several women who began applying what they perceived as the healing aspects of dance to work with people who had severe psychological disturbances (Levy, 1992). Over the years since then, many dancers have been drawn to the field through their own healing experiences with dance, forming a passionate, artistic, and ethical professional body. Dance/movement therapy is offered to groups and individuals of all ages, with many different diagnoses and other emotional, developmental, cognitive, and/or psychospiritual reasons for seeking help. The desire to safely share the power of dance has led to the standardization of extensive graduate-level training that includes theory and practice of psychotherapy methods. Thus we find ourselves straddling two professional cultures: dance and psychology.

SCIENCE. Patti Lather, a qualitative researcher, who has written from a feminist, poststructuralist position, has "asserted that science must be a process that stimulates a movement from established knowledge toward that which lies beyond the existing boundaries of conception" (McGettigan, 1997, p. 369). This broad description accentuates discovery, expansion, and revolution. Science that sounds so much like art relieves some of the tension of the imagined polemic between them. Nisbet states the similarities even more strongly:

> Not only is there no conflict between science and art, but . . . in their psychological roots they are almost identical. The unity of art and science exists most luminously in the motivations, drives, rhythms, and itches which lie behind creativeness in any realm, artistic or scientific. (1976, p. 4)

This recognition of similarities between art and science is somewhat comforting from within the interdisciplinary location of this investigation and of dance/movement therapy. Paradoxically, however, the task of this work is to clarify distinctions between scientific and artistic methods as well as to ease the rigidity around the definition of research as necessarily scientifically based.

For the purposes of understanding artistic inquiry as operationally distinct from "scientific" research methods, I will attempt to briefly clarify philosophical and methodological distinctions of science. Philosophically, positivist science has held that there is one absolute reality or truth, and that research of a certain kind will contribute toward knowing that truth. Traditional science also holds that discovering even small consistent pieces and patterns, and the recognition of rules regulating these consistencies will eventually add up to a unifying principle. Science as we know it today is primarily identified with two ways of knowing: empirical (that which can be apprehended by the senses or technological extensions of them) and analytic/logical.

Methodologically, science relies on empirical observation for initial data; inductive reasoning for the development of hypotheses; experimental testing for substantiation of these observations; statistical analysis to assess the validity of the findings; and further inductive reasoning to develop theory appropriate to the findings. Deductive reasoning can then be used to apply these generalized theories to particular cases.

THE RELEVANCE OF TRUTH TO ARTISTIC INQUIRY

In considering artistic forms of research, our assumptions and associations about both art and science are evoked and forced together. It is essential to be clear about how this influences our readiness to accept artistic inquiry as a form of research. One such association challenges our beliefs about the relevance of truth to research in general and artistic inquiry in particular.

When stretching the definition of research, as this work does, it also seems necessary to address the question of the nature of truth, as its pursuit has often been identified as the central purpose of research. It is possible to align with current postmodern thought and claim that there is no such thing as truth per se; that all truths are social, cultural, political, or personal constructions. It follows then that truth cannot be assessed with any certainty and so other constructs, such as meaning, understanding, or authenticity are more appropriate goals for research efforts. This is indeed a very compelling argument and very much in line with contemporary academic thinking.

However, truth is compelling in our everyday lives. Many of us are concerned with "reality" and want to know that our perceptions in some way correspond with what is "real." At times we long to know that there is truth that provides meaning and order to life, even if our limitations prohibit us from perceiving it. This begs the endlessly posed but ultimately unanswerable question of whether it is our subjective consciousness or some objective, material phenomena that are "real." Regardless of our position on this question, for many of us, belief in and the search for some form of universal truth continues to have relevance to our lived experience. I therefore feel justified in briefly addressing several conceptualizations of truth in association with research.

I am working from the assumptions that there are multiple ways of understanding the theoretical concept of truth and that there are many ways of pursuing and discerning truth in lived experience. Researchers are going to hold a variety of convictions about truth, and I believe that artistic inquiry may have more value for some than for others. Accordingly, I will discuss several ways of understanding truth that I believe are most relevant to those who might use artistic inquiry.

UNIVERSAL TRUTH. The traditional scientific or positivist idea of truth is that it is universal and absolute. This understanding, typically adhered to in the physical sciences and mathematics, rests on the philosophical assumption that absolute truth, or *a prior* knowledge, exists *independent* of subjective sensory experience. It is inborn and universal and makes absolute science possible. The scientific method, which (paradoxically it seems) uses sensory evidence in combination with logical reasoning, has come to be understood as the most dependable revelator of truth. Yet in this century, through the same scientific method, the existence of an "objective" reality has been challenged at the most basic level by evidence from new physics. As Fritjof Capra put it, "Twentieth century physics has shown us very forcefully that there is no absolute truth in science, that all our concepts and theories are limited and approximate" (1982, p.57).

Another kind of truth upheld by some to be as (or more) absolute and universal as that upheld by science is of divine origin. The methods of revealing this kind of truth are, however, radically different. Whereas science would depend on empirical evidence and human logic, divine Truth is apprehended through the authority of religion, sacred texts, or prophetic revelation directly from God (Herschel, 1962). Interestingly, scientific and spiritual seekers seem to have a dynamic attraction to one another's truths in their devotion to a unifying theory, as is evidenced by the recent upsurge of dialogues between scientists and theologians (Begley, 1998; Johnson, 1998).

There have also been artists that worked within the realms of both kinds of absolute truths. Seurat, for example, devoted his life to what he considered the scientific pursuit of understanding light as the absolute reality, and William Blake created prophetic poetry and images with what he felt was divine inspiration as his primary source. It is conceivable then that there are those who might pursue absolute scientific or divine truth through artistic inquiry.

INDIVIDUAL TRUTHS. In contrast to universal truths are those thought of as particular or pertaining to individual persons or situations. Some individual truths are based on purely subjective experience and need not correspond to anyone else's sense of reality. Yet they can be absolutely true for the individual regardless of their context. Another kind of particular truth is context-dependent and may be true for all people while they are in that context, but not outside of it. Social constructivism eschews the idea of any universal truth and adheres to a reality that "can only be understood through consciousness, through symbolic systems created and inscribed by historically situated humans" (Diversi, 1998, p. 133). Qualitative research is by definition performed within a paradigm that subscribes to this subjective conceptualization of reality and therefore, ascertaining truth is not the desired product. Instead, greater *understanding* of a particular person or group's experience of a phenomenon is the purpose.

ART AND TRUTH. Art's position is not easily located in this dialogue between absolute scientific truth and the social construction of reality. Although seemingly more compatible with a constructivist worldview, aesthetic, artistic, or poetic truth reflects a different, perhaps parallel or paradoxical position in relation to truth. There are also many different schools of thought regarding truth in art, and I will touch on several significant ones as they relate to artistic inquiry.

The simplest truth associated with art is representational truth, which is reflected in art that most literally resembles that which is being represented. However, many artists and aestheticians would suggest that truth conveyed by art lies beyond appearances or below the aesthetic surface. Just where below the surface this expression of truth dwells and how it is revealed has been the concern of philosophical treatises by Kant, Schopenhauer, Heidegger, Hospers, and Kandinsky, to name a few.

A fitting way to understand art's special relationship to truth is through metaphor. Making art has been imagined as opening a door, shedding a light, lifting a veil, holding a mirror, unfolding or piercing through to truth. These images all share the quality of revelation, or what Martin Heidegger would call "truth as unconcealedness of beings" (1971/1976, p. 678). In what I consider one of the most profound discussions on the subject, *The Origin of The Work of Art*, Heidegger described the creative process of the artist as "the becoming and happening of truth" (p. 694).

There are those, like contemporary sociologist Margerete Sandelowski, who point to the value of artistic truths that reveal something different than what we think scientific truths do.

> Interestingly, artistic truths are often more true to life than scientific ones, providing us with visions of human nature more resonant with our own experiences than any psychological, sociological or conventionally scientific rendering of it. (1994, p. 52)

Often times art serves to challenge or literally destroy old truths: "It serves to open thought rather than close it down. It helps us entertain possibilities - enriching or threatening - which may 'bring newness into the world'" (Steiner, 1995, p. 211).

Some, like Jacques Barzun, feel that "it is the duty of art to make us imagine the *particular*" (emphasis added, 1973, p.115) and see this as art's only authentic purpose. Others, like aesthetician Theodore Greene recognize revelation of the *universal* as art's ultimate contribution:

> The more significant the artist, the stronger has been his conscious or unconscious preoccupation with some aspect of *universal* human experience and the more compelling has been his desire to employ artistic form as a vehicle not for mere self-expression but for what he has felt to be a true and revealing interpretation of some aspect of his environment. (emphasis added, 1940, p.81)

However, I appreciate what Kant, Heidegger and Schopenhauer have proposed instead, that art uniquely reveals the universal in the particular.

> Schopenhauer insists that art is the most *universal* presentation of reality, while at the same time the most specifically sensuous presentation. It is this paradoxical joining of the sensuous and the universal which accounts for art's power and gratification. (emphasis added, Hofstadter & Kuhns, 1976, p. 447)

Dance critic Walter Sorrell metaphorically described this coexistence of the universal and particular in art as "the visualization or re-creation of that indefinable truth which the artist finds at one of the many crossroads between reality and his inner life" (1971, p. 17). What artistic inquiry has to offer dance/movement therapy is a method of discerning this kind of paradoxical, ineffable truth that we experience in our work and witness in the lives of our patients and giving it a form that can be shared with others.

DANCE AND TRUTH. We see the presence of juxtaposed individual and universal truths in the evolution of modern dance, which was the originating matrix for dance/movement therapy. Pioneering modern dancer and choreographer, Martha Graham's creative intention was to free dance from the elevated, stereotypical authority of ballet that suppressed the expression of individual truth. Eventually, however, she developed her own highly stylized technique with which to train the body as "an instrument with which to express great truths of life" (in Goellner & Murphy, 1995, p. 53). She created dances that revealed what she felt were universal and archetypal truths through dancers' bodies, exquisitely skilled in a very particular aesthetic.

Postmodern dance writer Sandra Horton Fraleigh described how, in contrast, later modern and postmodern choreography encouraged the expression of individuality for each dancer. She refered to increasing freedom from a stylized technique, resulting in a focus on unique movement styles and body types. She also described the essence of the paradoxical relationship between the personal and the universal:

> Her [the dancer's] individuality is present in tension with the universalizing impulse of the dance as it unites her self with other selves in understanding through the dance: Thus her individuality is engaged in surpassing self and is affirmed not as it sets her apart from others but as it becomes a binding element. The dancer transcends the limits of self in shedding her everyday persona, so characteristically and habitually assumed. She achieves this by consciously embodying the characteristic aesthetic qualities of each dance she performs. (1987, p. 30)

In Fraliegh's statement we can hear the essential manner in which client and therapist connect in dance/movement therapy. We understand one another through both the particular and the universal truths that are revealed through the dance. In dance/movement therapy we frequently see personal or particular truths expressed through dance or movement that is minimally formed and often cathartic, because the purpose is simply to express feeling spontaneously with the minimum of aesthetic and cognitive involvement. There are other times when client and therapist engage more aesthetic consciousness in a formative process resulting in movement more like a dance that intentionally expresses a more universally understood meaning. And, too, sometimes the persona of the dancer/client fades away to unconsciously reveal movement that clearly embodies a collective consciousness or archetypal message. In artistic inquiry about dance/movement therapy our challenge is to reveal and communicate both universal and particular truths about our work through the intentionally chosen aesthetic qualities of the particular dance (or other art form) that we present.

To summarize, truth as a concept is of essential significance to many potential researchers and consumers and is understood in different ways. If we choose not to adopt an exclusively scientific or social constructivist interpretation of truth, we are faced with the paradox of the coexistence of universal and individual truths. Art (and dance as an art form) is particularly well suited for expressing this paradox.

BEYOND TRUTH

Beyond truth, what does art have to offer as a mode of inquiry? Does it discover and communicate in unique ways that other forms cannot? There are those who assert that what art has to offer is unrelated to truth. "Asking whether a poem, painting, novel, or play is true is to ask the wrong question" (Eisner, 1991, p. 54). Jacques Barzun, in *The Use and Abuse of Art* (1973), pointed out how art has mistakenly tried to claim itself as a purveyor of truth, to be more like science. He described art as having recently adopted technical methods with inadequate results that compromise its integrity.

Douglas Morgan, in an essay entitled "Must Art Tell the Truth?" strongly stated, "In proclaiming that truths can be inferred from works of art we have really proclaimed very little, and nothing at all uniquely characteristic of art. For truths can be inferred from literally anything in the world" (1969, p. 225-226). Morgan asserted that to maintain that art deals in truth is to miss the fact that instead it offers the awakening of sensation, emotion, and imagination in ways that nothing else can. This awakening of the aesthetic, combined with the opportunity to authentically represent the most profound aspects of our work, is what artistic inquiry offers beyond truth.

AESTHETIC EXPERIENCE. Art offers an aesthetic experience, which according to cognitive researchers and theorists Csikszentmihalyi and Robinson,

> . . . occurs when information coming from the artwork interacts with information already stored in the viewer's mind. The result of this conjunction might be a sudden expansion, recombination, or ordering of previously accumulated information, which in turn produces a variety of emotions such as delight, joy, or awe. . . . The information in the work of art fuses with information in the viewer's memory—followed by the expansion of the viewer's consciousness, and the attendant emotional consequences. (1990, p. 18)

The aesthetic experience has been described as cognitive, perceptual, emotional, and spiritual (Csikszentmihalyi & Robinson, 1990) and could therefore be understood as one impacting most dimensions of human consciousness. Those familiar with dance and music would probably argue that the aesthetic experience is also kinesthetic, making it veritably holistic. Artistic inquiry, if it offers its audiences an aesthetic experience, can be understood as communicating information holistically rather than only analytically or empirically.

The aesthetic characteristics of artistic inquiry will be addressed further in Chapter 5.

AUTHENTICITY.   Guba and Lincoln (1989) introduced the term "authenticity" as an alternative to the positivist concept of "validity" to refer to a credibility criterion that reflects the values of the naturalistic or constructivist research paradigm. It refers to the intentional representation of the realities of all who are involved in the design, methodology, and presentation of the research. They expressed special concern for the accurate representation of the realities of the group traditionally referred to as "subjects," as these were most often misrepresented or subsumed under the worldview of the researchers. In proposing artistic inquiry as an alternative research approach, I am as much concerned about the authentic representation of the realities of researchers whose worldviews have been oppressed by an ill-fitting paradigm that does not reflect their values, ways of knowing, and unique skills. Similar concern for the authentic involvement of the researcher is reflected in this insightful comment by art therapists Junge and Linesch:

> Crucial to effective and enjoyable research for the art therapist is that there
> be a match between his or her personal style of engaging with the world and
> the particular research methods utilized in the inquiry. (1993, pp. 62-63)

To return to truth just briefly, Frederich Nietzsche and later Michel Foucault both suggested that truth is basically a commodity, and that its value is in the power it gives those who can claim it (Sheridan, 1980). From this perspective, the pursuit of truth and knowledge through research is about aspiring toward power. It is easy to see the evidence of this viewpoint in the reasons commonly given for doing quantitative or traditional scientific research: jobs, money, and professional acknowledgment. Certainly these are demonstrations of power that have value to most working professionals, and research may in fact help secure them. As Shaun McNiff wrote, "Scientific validity is essentially a matter of what people believe to be true, useful, and in their personal interest" (1986, p. 280).

But let me suggest just a few other things that I believe most dance/movement therapists also value: relationship, embodiment, creativity, dance, sensation, action, play, intuition, wholeness, empathy, authenticity, emotion, metaphor, imagination, healing, beauty, the unconscious, and the spirit. Though it would be difficult to put a numerical or monetary value on any of them, these are what make dance/movement therapy uniquely what it is. Artistic inquiry is a form of research that engages and reveals these phenomena more directly than scientific methods ever could, and so *authentically* reflects some of the more qualitative values of the profession. McNiff quoted philosopher Rudolf Carnap as saying:

> Let us learn from the lessons of history. Let us grant to those who work in any special field of investigation the freedom to use any form of expression which seems useful to them; the work in the field will sooner or later lead to the elimination of those forms which have no useful function. (in McNiff, 1986, p. 280)

Could it be that the reason quantitative research methods have not taken off in dance/movement therapy, as some hoped they would and claim they need to, is that they do not serve a useful function to those who might engage them? If we think of the construction of knowledge as the process of building a world that is meaningful to us, could it be that quantitative methods simply do not address this purpose, and so have little relevance? In reference to the kind of knowledge building that researchers do:

> Kant thinks of us as artists at play: we imagine and paint a subject, all the while enjoying the work we do because *of seeing our values realized within it*. (emphasis added, Weissman, 1993, p. 5)

Whatever research methods we choose need to realize our authentic values or else they will bring us no joy, no intrinsic reward, no meaning, and no power.

Methods of inquiry also need to engage the researchers' epistemologies to yield the best results. I am assuming that a high proportion of dance/movement therapists' primary ways of knowing are those necessary for successful practice of their chosen profession.

These would be described by Howard Gardner's Multiple Intelligences Theory (Gardner, 1985) as interpersonal, intrapersonal, spatial, musical, and bodily-kinesthetic. At least the first two of these are highly subjective modes not valued by the dominant research paradigm that relies heavily on linguistic and logical-mathematical epistemologies. The ways of knowing used by dance/movement therapists can also be described as aesthetic, poetic, or artistic (Allen, 1995; Eisner, 1985b; Junge & Linesch, 1993; Nisbet, 1976; Taylor, 1998); intuitive (Bastick, 1982; Hawkins, 1991; Noddings & Shore, 1984; Polanyi, 1966; Shallcross & Sisk, 1989); extrasensory (Rubick, 1996; Talbot, 1991); spiritual (Adler, 1992; Serlin, 1993); subjective and constructed (Belenky, Clinchy, Goldberger, & Tarule , 1986); and feeling based (Mitroff & Kilmann, 1978; Politsky, 1995).

This is not to claim that dance/movement therapists never use the ways of knowing favored by traditional science, (linguistic and logical-mathematical), but rather to suggest as Barzun did (1973) about artists, that these are not the primary strengths of many. The formal research has not been done to verify this claim about the primary ways of knowing of my colleagues, and it would be very valuable to the profession if it were. I base this assertion on almost 15 years of educating dance/movement therapy students in research and other areas; on presenting and discussing these ideas at many professional conferences; and on the required backgrounds of dance/movement therapists in the arts and human services. My belief about the ways of knowing of creative arts therapists is further supported by the writings of Gantt (1986), McNiff (1993), Junge and Linesch (1993), Landy (1993), Politsky (1995) and Edwards (1993).

Artistic inquiry has the potential to engage the professional skills of the dance/movement therapist that are uniquely different from those of colleagues such as social workers, verbal counselors, occupational therapists, psychologists, or psychiatrists. Some of these skills we share with other creative arts therapists, such as aesthetic sensitivity and understanding how to participate fully in and facilitate the creative process. Other skills are developed specifically through training in dance and dance/movement therapy, such as heightened perception and description of movement, kinesthetic empathy, the creation of dance and expressive movement, and the formation of relationship through movement.

Art, like other methods of expressing our perceptions of the world and the meanings we make, reflects our whole range of beliefs, attitudes, values, and ideas. The personal styles of dance/movement therapists are deeply informed by the artistic medium in which they have trained and express themselves: the dancing body (Bruno, 1990). The creative arts therapeutic process is likewise infused with the creative process of the arts (Landy, 1993). It seems natural then for the research process to also reflect the artistic and creative natures of the profession. It is my hope that with the acknowledgment and promotion of an alternative way of doing research and the demonstration of its potential to communicate the essence of our work, that dance/movement therapists will welcome the opportunity to exercise their creative research abilities. It is my firm belief that we have strengths in embodied, artistic, and aesthetic ways of knowing that are inherent in our work, and that these epistemologies can be authentically applied to research. I do not mean to say that dance/movement therapists are not capable of producing scientific research, only that it may not always be the most suitable paradigm for our purposes. It is also not my intention to supplant the admirable efforts being made to produce scientific research, but only to offer another option that hopefully will empower more clinicians to document the essential qualities of their work that they find valuable and viable. As Elliot Eisner has recently written,

> Methods and aptitudes interact. Not every research form is good for every player. The availability of qualitative research methods in the fullness of their possibilities offers researchers opportunities to select a way of working that fits their interests, is congruent with what they wish to study, plays to their strengths, exploits their aptitudes, and gives them a chance to find a place in the sun. (1997, p. 264)

Chapter 2

LITERATURE REVIEW

INTRODUCTION

BECAUSE RESEARCH IS AN interdisciplinary phenomenon, this review draws from several fields of human inquiry in which there have been acknowledgments of the potential and practice of research using artistic methods. This includes a small selection from creative arts therapies, psychology, and organizational development and a more significant body of literature from education and the social sciences. My focus is on the attempts by proponents in each field to define and validate research that uses artistic methods. In my estimation, the two contributors with the greatest value to dance/movement therapy are Shaun McNiff and Elliot Eisner, whose writings on the topic will therefore receive the most attention.

The recognition of artistic inquiry has been advanced by the growing acceptance of research methods variously referred to as qualitative, naturalistic, constructivist, or phenomenological in the social sciences and education. For thorough descriptions of the evolution of these methods I refer readers to two rich resources: Amedeo Giorgi (1986) who focused primarily on the tension between the arguments for scientific objectivity and a more humanistic approach in the social sciences; and Renata Tesch (1990) who provided a very thorough and insightful interdisciplinary overview of the history of qualitative research.

RESEARCH IN DANCE/MOVEMENT THERAPY

In 1981, the American Dance Therapy Association's Annual Conference was entitled "Research as a Creative Process." Interestingly, the compendium of 63 abstracts contains only one, by Arthur Leath, that gave any indication of research being understood as anything resembling creative. One abstract suggested the need for creative solutions to particular research problems, but did not elaborate on this simple declaration. Another, submitted not by a dance therapist but by a nurse, recognized the "exciting and creative" shift in the research paradigm, referring to the emergence of a qualitative approach (p. 2). Many presentations were descriptions of quasi-experimental projects, several were either purely theoretical or integrated theory and practice by describing programs or cases, and two were of a qualitative nature. This representation of research methodologies is not unusual for the human sciences at that time, but I found the contradiction between the title of the conference and the content of its presentations typical of the conflict still present within dance/movement therapy's professional psyche. Somewhere in the formative phases of this conference, someone recognized the potential for research to be creative, but in the actual manifestation, the creative element was all but missing.

Based on two annotated bibliographies covering dance/movement therapy literature up to 1990 (Fisher, 1992; Fledderjohn & Sewickley, 1993), and a search of the computer database, PsychLit, the overwhelming majority of books, articles, theses, and dissertations are theoretical or descriptive of theory in practice. The next largest category contains traditional case studies and quasi-experimental projects. A minor smattering of interviews, surveys, content analyses, and a mixture of other quantitative and qualitative methods make up the small body of remaining literature. In the past ten years I have read a few master's theses that use heuristic and artistic methods to explore various students' experiences in training and early clinical work that come closest to meeting the criteria for artistic inquiry. There is only a small handful of articles written about research methodology, all of which support quantitative, treatment-outcome methods. There is only one work, a book edited by a dance/movement therapist but addressing the creative arts therapies in general, that contains three essays supporting qualitative methods (Payne, 1993). One of these in particular, by dance/movement therapist Bonnie Meekums, finally draws well-articulated parallels between research and the creative process.

It is this context within which I am encouraging consideration of artistic inquiry as a viable alternative for dance/movement therapy research. Because we have no literature about artistic inquiry, I rely on the work of scholars from other fields to light the path toward this new possibility.

ARTISTIC INQUIRY IN THE CREATIVE ARTS THERAPIES

> Ill-equipped either by temperament or by training to undertake rigorous empirical investigations following the research model of the natural sciences...art therapists do not venture beyond the individual case study. (Gantt, 1986, p. 111)

With this disparaging statement, art therapist Linda Gantt identified the sadly limited state of research methodology in her field in 1986 and suggested alternative qualitative methods borrowed from anthropology, art history, and linguistics. The three analytical methods she offered were all descriptive and interpretive, using art products as data, but not focusing on the artist, art making, or the therapeutic process.

In the same year, Shaun McNiff, outspoken educator and leader in the creative arts therapies, implied in his first article on the subject, that "the long term interests of the profession will be advanced by the creation of research methods that emerge from the artistic process" (1986, p. 279). Although McNiff acknowledged the value of traditional research methods for some questions in the creative arts therapies, he began suggesting what the characteristics of an alternative kind of inquiry might be. He indicated that "a key element of art oriented research is respect for the emergence of meaning as a result of a relationship between researcher and the phenomena under consideration," (1986, p. 282) which in many cases is some form of art product or art making. He also suggested that "it is not unreasonable to encourage our scholars to apply the aesthetic principles of the profession to scholarship" (p. 283). Although these implications are somewhat vague, they do suggest artistic methods of data analysis that are guided by aesthetic values.

McNiff concluded this first article about research with a decree and a warning:

> When there is freedom of form, freedom of thought, and the opportunity to channel passion into scholarship, then research can be perceived as *artistic inquiry*. When institutions, professions, and communities begin to expect all research to follow prescribed formulas of operation then scholarship loses its artistic soul and knowledge is limited to what is contained within the prevailing articles of faith. (emphasis added, 1986, p. 283)

The "articles of faith" to which he refers are the assumptions that adherents to a particular paradigm, in this case that of the behavioral sciences, accept as true.

The following year, McNiff wrote more specifically as to what research in the creative arts therapies would actually look like if it were to "establish philosophical attitudes toward research that promote variety and methods of inquiry that fit the artistic mission of the profession" (1987, p. 285).

He made the recommendation that interdisciplinarity be considered when looking for research methods to use as models because "within the creative arts therapies and the history of depth psychology, interdisciplinary cooperation has been the norm rather than the exception. Virtually all of the scholars who have had a formative influence on our profession have mixed disciplines" (p. 285). I assume, based on the context of this and his previous article, that he is recommending that researchers look beyond the behavioral sciences for their methodology.

After commenting briefly on the usefulness of statistics and historical research methods for some inquiries, he went on to introduce the works of Rudolf Arnheim and of James Hillman as exemplary of artistic inquiry. He acclaimed Arnheims' research on making and perceiving art works "for its longstanding and primary commitment to art, and his respect for the artist, the image, and the dynamics of the artistic process" (1987, p. 289). McNiff saw Hillman's contribution as his unique treatment of images as vital entities with lives of their own. The description of Hillman's work foreshadowed McNiff's later explication of "image dialogue" as a method for research and therapy (see Chapter 3, section on Artistic Data Analysis).

In one of his more illuminating recommendations, McNiff suggested that artistic inquiry could free research from linearity the way the novel "was transformed through the methodological revolutions of writers like James Joyce who introduced contrasting ways to deal with time, space, structure, and language" (McNiff, 1987, p. 290). To do this, "imaginative inquiry" could use "poetic expression, narrative and dialogue" (p. 290).

Before ending his article with a series of recommendations, McNiff expressed a concern about the poor use of art in the name of research:

> I have witnessed many well-intentioned studies that present unintelligible, fragmented, and loosely associated materials as examples of artistic inquiry. The methods of art demand discipline and skill. As we begin to apply the arts to research and scholarship our efforts should be guided by assurances that what we do will be of use to others within the larger professional community. (McNiff, 1987, p. 288)

Unfortunately, it is not hard to imagine the kind of unintelligible research McNiff is referring to, given the kind of guidelines that creative arts therapists have had by which to conduct this new kind of inquiry. In the final suggestions that he offered (see next paragraph), he identified the "illusive" nature of these methods. It is precisely this difficulty that I hope to remedy.

McNiff concluded "Research and Scholarship in the Creative Arts Therapies" by recommending "a research tradition that supports variety in its scholarly methods and realms of inquiry" (1987, p. 291) and an interdisciplinary perspective that integrates the arts, humanities, and sciences. He hoped that these innovative kinds of research would "not only serve the practical needs of our emerging profession, but also attract attention from outside the discipline" (p. 291). He envisioned that future researchers would use "the arts as modes of empirical inquiry to contribute to the expansion of behavioral science research," ("empirical" meaning a method that relies on sensory perception as its primary resource) (p. 291). He recommended expansion of the scholarly Western tradition into "realms of knowledge and experience that can be grasped only through forms that correspond to their passion, complexity, and illusiveness" (p. 291). Like Arnheim, he felt creative arts therapy research should have "'the smell of the studio,' stay close to the practice of art and the statements of artists, respect images, and allow them [the images and/or the artists?] to present themselves in ways native to their being" (p. 291). And finally, as if looking back over his shoulder, he recommended "applying existing psychological theory to the arts," while looking forward to creating "original theory, indigenous to art" (1987, p. 291).

Although this article most directly addressed McNiff's concerns about the state of research in the creative arts therapies, the reader is still left with less than a clear sense of how to go about fulfilling these philosophically ambitious, yet vague directives.

In the final article of the three that he wrote specifically about research, "The Authority of Experience" (1993), McNiff declared himself a "practitioner researcher" and essentially discouraged any kind of research in the creative arts therapies that was not consistent with the values and methods of its practice. He opened, "I have always been uncomfortable with the assumption that research in creative arts therapy can only be conducted according to scientific procedures." (p. 3). He pointed out the inconsistencies between the profession's attitudes toward research and practice: "We have analyzed free expression with the fixed ideas that both creative science and art consider inimical to discovery and in-depth inquiry" (p. 3). He cited a lack of imagination and spontaneity, and offered art therapists Helen Landgarten and Bruce Moon as exemplary researcher practitioners whose works convey universality through empathy. Overall, what McNiff conveyed best was a sense of inspiration through championing the values and methods of his profession, but fell short of providing clear guidelines, at least in these published forums, for researchers wanting to pursue their own artistic inquiry. *

In 1993, the leading journal of the creative arts therapies, *The Arts in Psychotherapy* published a special issue on research in which authors from several disciplines acknowledged or encouraged the use of qualitative research methods. It opened with "A Research Agenda for the Creative Arts Therapies" by its editor, Robert Landy, a drama therapist, who reminded his readers that creative arts therapy is "first and foremost, aesthetically-based" (p. 1). He asserted that "the time has come to challenge not only the reigning positivistic approaches to research in the social sciences but also our own limited imaginations in regard to an understanding of research" (p. 2).

To back up this declaration Landy provided an agenda with seven

---

* Since that time, McNiff has published a definitive work that fills in the gaps left by his previous writings. McNiff's ever-evolving ideas are explicated in *Art-Based Research* (1998) through extensive examples of research using the art process as their primary methodology.

points expressed in general terms, three of which were applicable to artistic inquiry in particular, rather than more broadly to qualitative research. He felt the profession should be "framing researchable questions that are germane to the aesthetic nature of the creative arts therapies and that lead to an uncovering of the healing properties of the creative arts" (1993, p. 1). He suggested the addition of "aesthetic research" to a list of research categories generated by Junge and Linesch, (who I discuss next) "wherein the researcher documents and/or analyzes his or her creative process while engaged in creating an artwork for therapeutic purposes" (pp. 1-2). He also proposed that "the means of analysis/description should reflect the aesthetic nature of the research" (p. 2).

In the same issue, art therapists Junge & Linesch (1993) and music therapist Forinash made very articulate and well supported arguments for the use of qualitative research methods "to examine and further understand the often complex and enigmatic aspects of our clinical practice that cannot adequately be addressed by quantitative research" (Forinash, 1993, p. 69). Although both articles acknowledged the artistic, creative nature of the clinical work in their fields, neither explicitly recommended artistic methods of research as distinct from qualitative or phenomenological. In 1995, Politsky covered similar ground, referring to the work of Mitroff and Kilmann (1978), who developed a typology of research styles based on a Jungian model. Her central claim was that creative arts therapists embody the antithesis of analytical scientism and are best suited to doing phenomenological studies that embrace a postmodern aesthetic of "the impure, ambiguity, contradiction, complexity, incoherence and inclusiveness" (p. 312).

In a book edited by dance therapist Helen Payne (1993), rare in its devotion entirely to research in the creative arts therapies, contributors also suggested alternatives to quantitative methods to remedy the paucity of research they saw in the field. In attempts to make research seem more compatible to clinical practice, Meekums (1993) recognized research as a creative process, and Meekums and Payne (1993) described a type of research that could be done without resorting to measurement and reductionism (illuminative evaluation). Again, these authors did not advocate specifically for artistic methods of inquiry, but encouraged movement away from the exclusivity of the quantitative paradigm.

In further support of research and theory building that is "art indigenous," expressive arts therapists Knill, Barba and Fuchs (1995) presented five phenomenological research methods that they applied specifically to work in the creative arts therapies: hermeneutic, art indigenous analysis, dialogue transcripts, aesthetic methods, and metaphorical methods. All of these use methods compatible with research in dance/movement therapy, but only one, dialogue transcripts, meets the defining characteristics of artistic inquiry. (See a further description of dialogue transcripts in Chapter 3.) They concluded that when doing research on the expressive arts in therapy, "the only responsible approach available to us is an evocative, exploratory, poetic one, one which utilizes art to study art" (1995, p. 162).

ARTISTIC INQUIRY IN PSYCHOTHERAPY AND PSYCHOANALYSIS

Psychoanalysts, particularly Jungian, have traditionally used references to patient art to enrich case studies through what Knill et al. would call metaphorical methods. Rarely are the art works understood aesthetically, and they are most often interpreted through the theoretical framework of the analyst. Methods of inquiry are not usually described explicitly, but are assumed to be the interpretive methods used in a standard psychoanalysis. Edward Edinger (1990), whose work will be described in Chapter 3 published an excellent example of this kind of inquiry.

A group of researchers from the United Kingdom, in fields related to psychotherapy and behavioral sciences, formed an innovative research study group out of which came two books, *Human Inquiry* (Reason & Rowan, 1981) and *Human Inquiry in Action* (Reason, 1988). Both explored cooperative research methods, some of which were artistic and all of which were sensitive to an evolving, creative, collaborative process among research participants. In particular, Reason and Hawkins (1988) in "Storytelling as Inquiry" described a method in which stories were created about a phenomenon to understand it. Rather than using a more traditional narrative analysis to then gain further insight, stories about the original story were created by coresearchers in an ongoing cooperative "dialectic of expression" (p. 95).

Reason and Hawkins clarified a distinction between two basic methods of inquiry: explanation and expression.

"Explanation is the mode of classifying, conceptualizing, and building theory from experience" (1988, p. 79), and takes the forms of descriptive analysis or experimentation. In contrast, "expression is the mode of allowing the meaning of experience to become manifest" (p. 80) and often happens through a creative arts medium. It is this later method that is used in artistic inquiry, as is evidenced in Reason and Hawkins' further description of the languages and forms used:

> There are many languages in which meaning can be created and communicated: the languages of words which lead to stories and poetry; the languages of action which lead to mime, gesture, and drama [and dance]; the languages of colour and shape that lead to painting and sculpture; the languages of silence and stillness which are part of meditation. The languages are analogical and symbolic; they do not point out meaning directly; they demonstrate it by re-creating pattern in metaphorical shape and form. (1988, p. 81)

Similarly they distinguished between denotative thinking, which is scientific, and connotative thinking, which is "concerned with the Arts and the capacity of the human individual to create worlds and objects of polyvalent meanings: metaphors and symbols...Connotative thinking can be understood as the elaboration of feeling and emotional imagery and intuition into created form and expression" (Eckhartsberg in Reason & Hawkins, 1988, p. 82). These two sets of distinctions help clarify the nature of storytelling in particular, or artistic inquiry in general, and validate it as a way of knowing different from, and as they proposed, complementary to scientific inquiry.

Reason and Hawkins raised the provocative question, "When we tell stories, are we *creating* meaning or *discovering* it?" (p. 96), which seemed to challenge the reality and value of the meaning derived from their methods. They answered the challenge in three ways, all important to the discussion of artistic inquiry. First, from the perspective of archetypal psychologist R. Avens (1980), they proposed that what is "created" through our imaginations is as real and accessible in the collective psyche as anything that can be perceived or "discovered" through empirical means in the material world. Second, referring to the work of Ken Wilbur (1981), they pointed out the distinction between traditional modes of research in the realm of matter and unique modes of inquiry in the equally real realm of the psyche.

In a holistic view of knowing, matter, mind, and spirit interpenetrate: we have moved beyond the unreformed materialism of orthodox inquiry, and we need now to integrate a knowing from spirit (psyche, soul) with our existential human inquiry. A science of persons is inadequate without a knowing from soul. (Reason & Hawkins, 1988, p. 97-98)

Thirdly, they recognized David Bohm's (1980) theory of the implicate order in which the world in constantly unfolding and refolding, and what seems to be our creation is no different than discovery of what is unfolding due to our participation. All three answers led to the paradoxical resolve that "our meaning is simultaneously created by us and manifested through us" (Reason & Hawkins, 1988, p. 98).

Reason and Hawkins proceeded from these theoretical musings to several brief, but concrete and clear, explications of using storytelling as an artistic form of data analysis. In addition, Hawkins (1988) contributed a chapter to the same book in which he gave examples of psychodrama as another artistic method of data analysis.

ARTISTIC INQUIRY IN THE SOCIAL SCIENCES

Anthropology, a branch of social science, has since its inception used ethnography as its primary research methodology. Ethnographers have rarely attempted to quantify or statistically validate their findings. Frequently they have been concerned with the observation and description of the artistic process and product as a manifestation of culture. Other kinds of social scientists have adopted ethnographic methods, and as a result have been more open to a wide range of qualitative approaches. In the 1970s sociologists and anthropologists began acknowledging the philosophical and pragmatic similarities between research and art, and searching for ways to incorporate more of the artistic in their research (Brown, 1977; Clifford & Marcus, 1986; Geertz, 1983; Goldwater, 1973; Nisbet, 1976). These beginnings were articulately carried forth by others, including Sandelowski (1994), who revisited the relationship between art and science, reinforcing their commonalties in terms of creative motivation, the search for truth, and use of aesthetic criterion. She encouraged social science researchers to strive "toward a science that both acknowledges and celebrates its art" (p.49).

> Celebrating the art permits us to turn to nonscientific sources of knowledge (literature, art, and literary and artistic criticism) as data themselves and to use theory imaginatively (including theories of fiction, dance, and music) to frame and enhance analysis. Celebrating the art permits us to experiment with forms of representing findings that best reprise the experiences we wish to convey. (p. 56)

Social science researchers had been experimenting with artistic forms of representation, notably literary forms such as poetry, story and drama for some time when Sandelowski wrote her article. Laurel Richardson, a writer/researcher proponent of such literary research forms, in her contribution to the *Handbook of Qualitative Research* (1994) credits the postmodern context as contributing to this dilation of possibilities. She traces the separation of art and science back to the philosopher scientists of the seventeenth century, but cites numerous recent social science and literature crossovers, from Balzac and Zola, to a whole wave of postmodern, mixed-genre researchers published from 1981 to 1993. Richardson championed writing as a valid way of knowing and encouraged social scientists to make use of several literary methods to improve their work. Included were suggestions for how researchers could incorporate experimental writing and metaphor in their methodology. Richardson has published many theoretical and research works in support of what she called these "transgressive" research methods (1990a, 1990b, 1991, 1992, 1993, 1994, 1995, 1997).

Another prolific author, Jim Mienczakowski (1992, 1994a, 1994b, 1995a, 1995b, 1996; Mienczakowski, Smith, & Sinclair, 1996) has been a strong proponent for the use of dramatic or theatrical methods of inquiry, particularly in the service of social action. His interdisciplinary focus has expanded into areas of healthcare in several of his articles that described the use of ethnodrama and theatrical catharsis to create change in the health care of addiction and head-injury patients. These topics make his work an especially valuable resource to dance/movement therapists who desire to give voice to their patients' experiences and to affect change in the settings within which they work.

Richardson and Mienczakowski have provided strong impetus to a postmodern wave of social scientists that are risking this transgressive, mixed-genre sea of inquiry methods. This is evidenced by more research articles than are practical to cite here that refer to these two authors' works as theoretical justification for the methods used. These articles typically discuss methodology and demonstrate artistic methods of data analysis or presentation borrowed from poetry, autobiography, fiction, or drama. Recently Ellis and Bochner edited *Composing Ethnography*, the first in a series of books that "will emphasize experimental forms of qualitative writing that blur the boundaries between social sciences and humanities" (1996, p.2). They have gathered together examples of newly formed categories of research with hybridized names: *autoethnography, sociopoetics* and *reflexive ethnography*. The editors report that the response to their call for papers was overwhelming, and thus the series was conceived.

David Barry, another interdisciplinary scholar who has contributed to artistic inquiry in the social sciences, has researched within the field of organizational development. Barry's article, entitled "Artful Inquiry" (1996), explicated a method that he called symbolic constructivism, and should be of special interest to dance/movement therapists. His method is one used by many creative arts therapists, except that he effectively valorized it through the use of postmodern language commonly used in the academic social sciences. He used art (or other "non-routine portrayal") made by his clients (employees, managers, administrators) "to catalyze alternative knowings of conscious, tacit, and nonconscious beliefs and feelings" about their work situations (p. 411). The process he described, of meaning "intersubjectively constructed" and "arising from the interplay between inquiring parties" will be so familiar to therapist readers that it may be difficult to reframe what he has presented as research (p. 412). Barry acknowledged the use of "in vivo, respondent-generated symbol creation as a research method...being confined...to more psychologically oriented fields: art therapy, Jungian and Gestalt psychology, family therapy, and consumer perception research" (p. 413).

Of value to this discussion is Barry's recognition of the reasons that symbolic constructivism (SC) has been rarely used for research:

> Art-based methods tend to be intrusive, time consuming, resistance prone, confusing, frustrating, and dependent on the clinical skills of the researcher. The researcher may end up acting as interviewer, interviewee, theorist, creative director, materials expert, aesthete, hand-holding confidence booster, empathic listener, and occasionally therapist – a combination that can understandably land SC in the "too hard" pile. (p. 423)

Fortunately for dance/movement therapists, these are challenges they are accustomed to, trained to deal with, and skills they already use regularly. Barry described three kinds of inquiry incorporated in symbolic construction: *eliciting, revealing,* and *transforming.* Each is a level more challenging to the status quo of the participants, and therefore is more provocative of new awareness, leading to change.

In the following descriptions of methods, remember that Barry used them almost exclusively in corporate settings as a consultant, not as a therapist, and with the kind of functional, stable participants one would hope to find working there. *Elicitive* methods are used "if inquirers are mostly interested in evoking existing schemas and narratives, triggering forgotten [not repressed] memories, finding more compelling ways to frame current understandings, or wish to gently rock but not capsize the boat" (p. 423). *Revealing* methods are used to "explore the tacit or nonconscious aspects of the situation" (p. 425). (Barry does provide some ethical guidelines around dealing with repressed and therefore uncomfortable material, that do not, however, resolve for me the question of who should be doing this kind of research and under what conditions.) Finally, *transformational* methods are used when "everything is brought into question: Existing forms, meanings, and uses are challenged, new constellations suggested, and old ones changed or replaced" (p. 428). He concludes with a brief but detailed example, which seems much like a case study of a family or group art therapy session, except that the context is corporate and the goal is organizational change.

What Barry has contributed to social science is a method of using art forms other than literary as data and guidance as to how to understand data in a manner consistent with current constructivist research values. Because the goal of the work that Barry described, like dance/movement therapy, is to facilitate change, the focus of this article was on presenting a method for change. If adopted by others, its application and effectiveness could then become the focus of case studies. What Barry demonstrated for dance/movement therapists is a postmodern, constructivist reframing of a methodology we are already using. His methods may provoke the problem of distinguishing between therapy and research in the mind of the reader, but this is not addressed by the author.

ARTISTIC INQUIRY IN EDUCATION

Due primarily to the work of arts educator Elliott Eisner, there has been a substantial initiative toward arts-based research in education, especially in the area of educational evaluation. This movement is visible in educational research conferences, special interest groups within professional organizations, and in graduate level scholarship. A prolific author and outspoken leader, Eisner is a proponent for methods of evaluation and research that are congruent with artistic ways of knowing. He has published numerous articles in which over time he has refined and reframed his conceptualization of what he most recently has called arts-based research (1997). His article on the subject in 1981 outlined ten well developed dimensions of an artistic, in contrast to scientific, approach to qualitative research. At that time he was primarily referring to research presented through the written word, with suggestions that it might take other artistic forms. The 10 dimensions were:

- *The forms of representation employed.* "Artistic forms of representation place a premium on the idiosyncratic use of form – visual and auditory form as well as discursive form – to convey in nonliteral as well as literal ways the meanings the investigator wishes to express...What one seeks is not the creation of a code that abides to publicly codified rules, but the creation of an evocative form whose meaning is embodied in the shape expressed" (1981, p. 6).

- *The criteria for appraisal.* In contrast to validity in the sciences, "validity in the arts is the product of the persuasiveness of a personal vision; its utility is determined by the extent to which it informs...What one seeks is illumination and penetration" (p. 6).

- *Points of focus.* The focus of artistic approaches to research is on understanding experience and meaning. The way one accesses this understanding is "to 'indwell,' to empathize; that is to imaginatively participate in the experience of another...It is the content provided by this form of knowing that serves as a major source of understanding" (p. 6).

- *The nature of generalization.* "Generalization is possible [in artistic forms of inquiry] because of the belief that the general resides in the particular." An attempt is made "to shed light on what is unique in time and space while at the same time conveying insights that exceed the limits of the situation in which they emerge" (p. 7).

- *The role of form.* In scientific research, standardization of form is considered necessary. If there are any variations in form (and Eisner gives the example of the same test scores being displayed either numerically or graphically), the meaning of the content is not meant to change. "In artistic approaches to research, standardization of form is counterproductive. What artistic approaches seek is to exploit the power of form to inform...In short, form is regarded as a part of the content of what is expressed and bears significantly on the kinds of meanings people are likely to secure from the work" (p. 7).

- *Degree of license allowed.* "One of the strengths that artistically oriented research possesses is that liberties in portrayal are wider than they are in scientifically oriented studies . . . . [It] acknowledges what already exists and instead of presenting a façade of objectivity, exploits the potential of selectivity and emphasis to say what needs saying as the investigator sees it" (p. 8).

- *Interest in prediction and control.* "Artistically oriented research does not aim to control or produce formal predictive statements . . . . What it yields at its best are ineffable forms of understanding which can only by conveyed through the figurative or nondiscursive character of the artistic image which such research yields (see Langer, 1957)" (p. 8).

- *The sources of data.* "In artistic approaches to research, the major instrument is the investigator himself" (p. 8).

- *The basis of knowing.* "In artistic approaches to research, the role that emotion plays in knowing is central" (p. 8).

- *Ultimate aims.* In contrast to science, which is concerned with the discernment of truth, artistic approaches to research are concerned with meaning. Like art, they seek "the creation of images that people will find meaningful and from which their fallible and tentative views of the world can be altered, rejected, or made more secure" (p. 9).

Eisner ended this article by clarifying that his concern is with the promotion of methodological pluralism in the field of educational research, saying, "Our problems need to be addressed in as many ways as will bear fruit" (1981, p.9).

I turn next to what I consider Eisner's most significant work, *The Enlightened Eye: Qualitative Inquiry and the Enhancement of Educational Practice* (1991), in which he expanded on two concepts: *connoisseurship* and *criticism*, which he had introduced in at least two earlier articles (Eisner, 1976, 1977). Although he focused on the usefulness of these two methods in the evaluation of educational practices in particular, they have interdisciplinary relevance to artistic inquiry in that both are based on artistic or aesthetic skills.

Connoisseurship is "to notice or experience the significant and often subtle qualities that constitute an act, work, or object and, typically, to be able to relate these to the contextual and antecedent conditions" (Eisner, 1991, p.85). Although the term has connotations of exclusivity or elitism, Eisner's use of it intended to convey expertise through extended training and exposure. A connoisseur is someone in whose judgment one has confidence. The essential act of connoisseurship is discernment, but it does not necessarily include communication. Criticism, however, takes this next step: "to transform the qualities of a painting, play, novel, poem, classroom or school, or act of teaching and learning into a public form that illuminates, interprets, and appraises the qualities that have been experienced" (Eisner, 1991, p. 86).

To clarify the meaning of these terms and their value to artistic inquiry in dance/movement therapy I have constructed a hypothetical example. If I were interested in receiving some feedback as to the quality of the therapeutic relationships I was forming in my individual dance/movement therapy sessions, I might call on a supervisor whose expertise in the field was well demonstrated and in whose judgment I had confidence. If I showed her several videotapes of sessions and asked her for her feedback, she might be able to assess the quality of the therapeutic relationship based on the subtle and complex movement qualities she observed in each case. If she were a "connoisseur" of movement observation she might be able to tell me which session was most effective in developing the relationship. Her knowledge of movement analysis would allow her to make a reasonably reliable assessment as to what were the developmental or emotional issues of mine and the client's that contributed toward our successes or challenges. But unless she were also skilled in "criticism" she might not be able to convey in a rich and effective manner to a less informed audience, say students or administrators, what the determining qualities and their significance were. These expert skills of observation, analysis, and communication based on the artistic and aesthetic qualities of the art process and product could be applied to any therapy session in which art making in some form was central.

One of the most valuable contributions of *The Enlightened Eye*, is Eisner's attempt to explicate methods of determining the credibility of artistic approaches to research, which he called *structural corroboration, consensual validation,* and *referential adequacy.* Another unique aspect of this book is the inclusion of experiences from his own art making (he is a painter) and the writings of art critics and philosophers of art to build his readers' understanding of an aesthetic approach to doing research and an artistic way of knowing. His own description of the theoretical bases of artistic approaches to qualitative research is especially articulate, poetic, and convincingly supported.

In a special edition of *Educational Theory* (1995), devoted exclusively to the discussion of "artistically crafted research," Eisner's introductory article (which originated as a presidential address at the 1993 American Educational Research Association Conference), established three characteristics of an artistically crafted work. They are summarized here briefly:

> First, works of art make the obscure vivid and make empathy possible. Second, they direct our attention to individuality and locate in the particular what is general or universal. Third, they possess a sense of wholeness, coherence, and a kind of organic unity that makes both aesthetic experience and credibility possible. (Eisner, 1995, p. 4)

He then presented three characteristics of social science that are art-like. The first he termed *constructive neglect*, or the ability to attend away from that which is not essential to the guiding questions. The second is *imaginative extrapolation*, which "involves using what one sees to generate theoretical interpretations that give the particular situation a fresh significance" (Eisner, 1995, p. 4). The third is the process of being *artistically engaged*, which "rests upon the ability to negotiate the tension between control and surrender, between giving into the insistent demands of the world and yielding to the chaos of the unconscious" (p. 5).

In this essay, Eisner did not go so far as to advocate for nonverbal art forms as research, but continued instead to promote textual forms with the characteristics of poetry, novels, and plays. He did, however, provide a wider description of research that theoretically could include any art form. Stating that "the primary tactical aim of research is to advance understanding," he cited several novels that "help us understand because their creators understood and had the skills and imagination to transform their understanding into forms that help us notice what we have learned not to see. They provide an image fresh to behold, and in so doing provide a complement to the colorless abstraction of theory with renderings that are palpable" (1995, p. 3).

Eisner is not without opponents in the field of education, who hold more conservative views of what should pass for scholarly research in the field of education. One of the best known is Howard Gardner, who debated Eisner on the subject at the 1996 American Educational Research Association Conference on Qualitative Research Methods. Another is one of his Stanford colleagues, D.C. Phillips (1995), who made several strong arguments in direct response to Eisner's 1993 address and 1995 essay, cited above. It is important to note that most of these arguments are based on positivist assumptions and the equating of research with science. I will mention the points Phillip's makes that have challenged me to examine my understanding of artistic inquiry further and that I address within this book.

His first points of contention were in regard to Eisner's definition of research (an activity that advances understanding), which Phillips felt was bizarrely inclusive, and the claim that the arts enable us to discern meanings that other methods do not. He challenged Eisner to:

> Provide a criterion that would enable us to distinguish those works of art that are research from those that are not; it would also seem to be important for him to assist us in recognizing and evaluating the meanings that artists do discern, and to explain why these artistic meanings have relevance for the sorts of theoretical and policy questions that social scientists and other educational researchers are conducting research upon. (1995, p. 74)

He went on to claim that Eisner's artistic orientation had blinded him to the fact that "the nature investigated by scientists is not infinitely tolerant of the stories that are told about it!" (Phillips, 1995, p. 75). His argument was that artists can portray nature in any way they want, can impose whatever fantasies they can conjure, because they work within the unconstrained field of the imagination. He also argued against considering truth to be something other than propositional, and other than something that can be proven false.

Phillips also reminded his readers that "research is always directed toward solving specific problems" and that Eisner gives "no precise examples of the sorts of educational or social problems where this broadening [of methods] would be appropriate" (1995, p. 77). He expressed concern that the arts can and have been used for destructive purposes, as in influencing people emotionally through political propaganda, and if called "research" might add undeserved validity to their effectiveness. (I am reminded that science has been used more potently for worse purposes, and its supposed freedom from emotional involvement may have allowed the destruction to occur.)

But for me, the most provocative challenge that Phillips offers, and one that I believe, like his others, comes from a powerfully different world-view and is captured in this question:

> Why [is] a work of literature or a sensitive film, which promotes reflection and insight . . . somehow made stronger by being considered a piece of research in the social science sense? The competent practice of an art undoubtedly is a complex and demanding cognitive activity, but not all such activity is research . . . and nothing is gained by pretending it is. . . . The arts need no such artificial shoring-up. (Phillips, 1995, p. 74)

This question awoke in me a concern that in advocating artistic inquiry I might somehow be doing the arts a disservice. I cannot know if that is the case, and I don't know what Eisner's response to Phillips' question was or would be. I can say that my purpose is not to shore-up or validate art by calling it science, but by recognizing its value as art. I wish to invite an expansion of our understanding by including the arts as a means of communicating the discoveries of practitioners whose ways of knowing and working are artistic.

Despite opposition from within the academy, in education there are those students and professionals who, like me, heard a voice in the wilderness in Eisner's message and have picked up the banner and carried it forth. Most are still advocating arts-based research in experimental literary forms of presentation, of which I will describe a few that are most enlightening to the use of artistic inquiry in dance/movement therapy.

Susan Finley and Gary Knowles (1995) explored the relationship between their artist and researcher selves through a dialogue that was spatially arranged on the page with aesthetic considerations beyond those codified by most professional journals. (This flexibility in written form has become fairly common in journals like *Qualitative Inquiry* which publish alternative paradigm, interdisciplinary research.) In her dialogue with Knowles, Finley describes her suspension between roles, tasks and mediums:

> "Yes. I am an artist." And I can say, "Yes. I am a researcher." But I have also discovered that my researcher self and artist self are not separate. I am simultaneously artist-as-researcher and researcher-as-artist, whatever specific task I am engaged in. When I am building a collage of images of a person's life history, I have heightened awareness of which experiences were most defining in that person's life. Even the materials that I choose must in some way record the social and political life, even the personality. The art of collage is a search for visual images to re-present life; the art of research is the search for written images that equally represent life. Sometimes the images that I seek to represent life are the same, regardless of the medium, but at other times one or the other medium allows me greater expression. (1995, p. 131)

While Finley talked about herself as an artist in other mediums, as a researcher she still worked within the traditional textual imperative. So did Sara Lawrence-Lightfoot and Jessica Hoffmann Davis (1997), who recently published a very thick explication of a research methodology that the former has coined *portraiture*. Although Davis, as an artist, provided richly artistic metaphorical elaboration of the method, their approach remains purely literary. What they have delivered (like Finley and Knowles) is a deepening portrayal of the aesthetic, artistic and creative qualities of the research product and process. One of their central goals was to bridge the rigor of science with the aesthetics and symbolism or art.

Another pair of women who explored an artistic analogy of research but stopped at narrative representation were Oldfather and West (1994). They compared qualitative research to jazz and beautifully illuminated the method's creative, improvisational nature. Valerie Janesick (1994) did the same with dance as the guiding metaphor, but made no suggestions to incorporate dance or any other art forms into the actual research process. Donmoyer and Yennie-Donmoyer recognized the difficulty the profession was having moving beyond textual experimentation, and in their 1995 article suggested using reader's theater as a mode of data representation.

So efforts have been made to move beyond the textual representation of findings, but more challenging to convention is research that uses any artistic methods to *analyze* data. There is even very little educational research that uses any form of art *as* data. However, of special interest to dance/movement therapists are two articles written by dancers, one (Stinson, 1995) promoting the use of information from the body as data and in support of analysis, and the other (Blumenfeld-Jones, 1995) the use of the body and dance as forms of data analysis and presentation. Stinson, like Janesick, primarily uses dance as a metaphor for research, but she does advocate the use of kinesthetic empathy as a method of understanding oneself and others more fully in the service of research.

Blumenfeld-Jones, although he explored the possibilities of dance as a means of representation, also addressed dance as a way of knowing, and a way of making meaning of one's experience. The published article is a transcript of a presentation he made in which he integrated his own words about dance with actual dancing. Obviously, as readers, we miss the dancing and can only get the portion of his message that is conveyed verbally. Such are the difficulties of dance as a form of presentation in a scholarly forum that is text dominated. Despite this, Blumenfeld-Jones managed to convey some interesting ideas on how to think about dance as a form of research representation. He discouraged the use of dance as mimicry of events or people and described the abstract quality of dance:

> The dancer is about shaping the motion in ways that make kinetic sense to him in the light of the idea upon which he reflects... The dancer/choreographer is focused upon the variant meanings of motion as arranged in time and space and shape... The motion itself must be the meaning. (1995, p. 394)

One point Blumenfeld-Jones hoped to convey was the possibility of understanding dance as text and to remind us that we interpret even words, which are not as "transparent" as we think they are. We are always making interpretations, though dance may not be the medium we are accustomed to interpreting. Thus,

> What makes dance meaningful is the ways in which we read it and are

moved into the world at large in a new way; the experience of dance can move us beyond the immediate moment of motion...The narrative is meant to express the essence of a thing, idea, person, or whatever is being reflected upon. (1995, p. 398)

Perhaps because of the difficulties encountered when trying to write about dance, one of the most impermanent and least discursive art modalities, Blumenfeld-Jones article didn't have the accessibility of written expression that Eisner and some others have demonstrated. He closed, though, with two very clear directives for dance as a research medium in any field:

Our focus should be on how dance might extend, energize, and bring out previously unseen aspects of the objects of our interest. To accomplish this, the quality of the dance must be made paramount, which means design and execution must be excellent. (1995, p. 400)

To conclude the review of educational research literature relevant to artistic inquiry, I return to Elliot Eisner. He and Tom Barone contributed a chapter in *Complementary Methods for Research in Education* edited by Richard M. Jaeger (1997). They define arts-based research as having "certain aesthetic qualities or design elements" (p. 73). They explicate seven definitive features of arts-based research in literary form:

- *The creation of a virtual reality.* This doesn't refer to the complex image world created by a computer, but to those creations in any medium in which the *verisimilitude* of the image allows the viewer to recognize "some of the portrayed qualities from his or her own experiences and is thereby able to believe in the possibility—the credibility—of the virtual world as an analogue to the 'real' one" (1997, p. 74).

- *The presence of ambiguity.* This quality "encourages a multiplicity of readings and a variety of interpretations" by not presenting "a single closed answer to the dilemmas posed within the text" (p. 75).

- *The use of expressive language.*

- *The use of contextualized and vernacular language.* Writers may use thick literary description including the nontechnical or everyday language of those being studied.

- *The promotion of empathy.* "Empathic understanding is the result of an inquirer's achievement of intersubjectivity" (p. 77).

- *Personal signature of the researcher/writer.* "The author shapes the [virtual] reality in accordance with his or her own particular thesis, or controlling insight, which the text is composed to suggest...This tentative personal statement of the author also serves as a mediator for choosing what to include or exclude from the text" (pp. 77-78).

- *The presence of aesthetic form.* Arts-based research forms are created to suit the unique needs of the researcher in communicating her or his understanding of the phenomenon under consideration. Examples of literary arts-based formats that are commonly used are story, dialogue, and poem.

Barone and Eisner discouraged the polarization of categories of research into "scientific and artistic" or "quantitative and qualitative" and suggested perceiving research on a continuum with varying degrees of these artistic characteristics. At the artistic end of the continuum they included not only literary works, but also those using other mediums, with film being particularly noted. They concluded their chapter by addressing a few of the significant changes that would need to occur in the education of researchers if arts-based inquiry were to become an accepted method. These included training in aesthetic judgment and artistic skills for student researchers, and the inclusion of aesthetically informed faculty to evaluate their research.

For the present discussion, what is particularly exciting about these final points is that they indicate how close dance/movement therapy is to being able to include arts-based methods in their research repertoire. The profession has researchers, faculty, editors, and critics trained in the methods and aesthetics of dance who are "in the wings," already equipped to create and evaluate arts-based research.

SUMMARY

As yet there is no evidence that researchers in the field of dance/movement therapy have given consideration to artistic inquiry in any way comparable to researchers in the fields reviewed here. Not only is there no research demonstrating methods that could be identified as artistic, there is no scholarly dialogue on the subject in professional publications. The only forums for this discussion have been provided by me at several recent dance/therapy conferences. And yet the parallels between the theory and practice of dance/movement therapy and the research being done in other fields seem so obvious that artistic inquiry in dance/movement therapy must be all but imminent. In the following chapters, the three defining characteristics of artistic inquiry will be discussed in depth, with these parallels drawn out as clearly as possible.

Chapter 3

ARTISTIC METHODS OF GATHERING, ANALYZING AND PRESENTING DATA

INTRODUCTION

$\mathbf{A}$RTISTIC METHODS ARE ACTIONS that result in art. Therefore, the concept of artistic *methods,* as used in this context, does not refer simply to the *products* of these actions. Yet the products are inseparable from the making, (especially in the lively arts such as dance) and so are implicit in the term. To understand what artistic methods of inquiry are, the *work* of art, from inception to preservation, must be perceived as a whole. This understanding clarifies that simply using an art object as data does not make research artistic. Interpretation or analysis of an art object also does not constitute artistic inquiry. In addition, artistic inquiry is not the use of types of analysis developed in relation to an art form, but which are not part of the art-making process. Both art objects and the interpretation of art may be *part* of artistic inquiry, but are not sufficient alone to warrant its identification as such.

To illustrate, consider these three hypothetical examples of types of research that have been produced in psychiatry, psychology, and the creative arts therapies, that are *not* artistic inquiry:

- Over a period of several years, an art therapist collects the drawings of all his patients who are in early recovery from alcoholism and cocaine addiction. He analyses these drawings from a psy-

44

chodynamic perspective and constructs a theory differentiating alcoholism from cocaine addiction based on two different developmental profiles that emerge in the art works.

- A Jungian, psychoanalytic, expressive arts therapist examines the entire body of literature written by an eminent poet who was documented as having a mental illness during a particular phase of his writing career. She develops a personality profile for the poet based on the archetypal images that she perceives in his work over time and develops a theory explaining how he recovered from mental illness.

- To develop greater insight into ongoing difficulty she is experiencing in a particular group, a dance/movement therapist does a complete Kestenberg Movement Profile on herself and the group. She uses a video tape of a previously recorded, especially problematic dance/movement therapy session. She discovers a clash in movement qualities between herself and a very active male group member. Through understanding his unresolved developmental issues as evidenced in the Kestenberg Movement Profile, she develops strategies to work more successfully with that person.

None of the above forms of research involve *art-making* on the part of the researcher or the subjects in response to the research question, even though all three seem to use art in some part of the process. Art-making as data gathering, art-making as data analysis, or art-making as presentation of findings are the definitive aspects of artistic methods of research that will be proposed in this chapter.

I will explain "actions that result in art" further before considering artistic methods of data gathering, analysis, and presentation individually. Illustrations of each will again be drawn from "Dance/movement therapy students' feelings and attitudes about doing research" (see Appendix). In addition, three examples of artistic inquiry will be discussed as they illustrate aspects of the distinction between art as data and artistic methods of research. Robert Ziller's research subjects used artistic methods to gather data in the form of photographs, although Ziller never explicitly treated the data as art (*Photographing the Self,* 1990). Glesne, in "That rare feeling: Representing research through poetic transcription" (1997), collected nonartistic data and used poetic transcription as a method to analyze and present it. Edward Edinger

(1990) aesthetically displayed art/data as part of the presentation of findings, allowing it to reveal its own meaning artistically. In each case it will be demonstrated how the *actions* intrinsic to the research that resulted in art determine whether the inquiry can be considered artistic, regardless of the nature of the data itself.

ACTIONS THAT RESULT IN ART

How are actions resulting in art different from other random, playful, intentional, or functional human behaviors? The following is an excerpt from my 1997 journal that addresses this question.

> Dance is made from the raw material of human movement. Movement is that functional, natural, even accidental activity I participate in with my body. Movement just happens. Most of the time I am not conscious of it happening at all. But, when I pay attention, the movement then changes in my awareness. I separate myself enough from it to see it. I also perceive it consciously through my tactile, kinesthetic and proprioceptive senses. I become subject to it as an object. It is no longer just me – it is me doing it. Out of this awareness I have the opportunity to appreciate it. To say "Oh, I like the way that looks, or feels" or "I want to do that again." Then I have the opportunity repeat it, if I have the skills to recreate it the way I experienced it the first time. So, when I do it again, with intention, it is like a little performance, during which my awareness increases. I perceive it more clearly, my appreciation either increases or decreases. I discriminate. If my appreciation decreases, I adjust it, throw it out, or put it aside for later, just in case. If my appreciation increases, I keep it, use it, repeat it, develop it. If I am satisfied with how it's developed, I may choose to show it to someone else. I want to shine a light on it and say "Look here!" to others. I remove it from its original context and it becomes a separate or independent entity with value and worth beyond its original state of being. I put it in a dance or on a stage so that it can be appreciated by me and others repeatedly.

> My skill at recreating the movement and creating a new context for it will determine its ongoing effectiveness or power, and the appreciation that others will have for it. Due to lack of skill I could accidentally stumble onto a movement or image and be unable to recreate it effectively or powerfully. Therefore, I would be unable to move from awareness to appreciation to intentional-recreation for myself and others. It would be lost to me and that movement would never become a dance. My skill in the original perceptual act is also critical. If I don't notice it, it can never become a dance.

Let me transpose this movement-to-dance example to a work of art in another medium, say painting. I see an image, either in the environment, or in my imagination. It captures my interest, I recreate it, perhaps in a little sketch. I like some of what I see, and develop it into a more clear, larger, more detailed painting. I cycle through stages until I am satisfied with the product, and I call in finished. I frame it and hang it on the wall. This process can be seen in artistic creation in any medium, and differs from a work of craft, or a functional object, in that its function is not my primary concern, its appearance (or sound, as in music or poetry) is.

To summarize, for a thing (image, movement, sound, words, lump of clay) to become a work of art, the following steps are performed by a human being who has the necessary skills to perform them:

1. *Initial awareness:* Some image/idea is singled out from its original context as special for aesthetic reasons. ("I like the way that looks or feels.") In artistic inquiry, this fragment of consciousness is recognized because in some way, which the artist/researcher may not even be aware of, it addresses the research question. It feeds his or her curiosity.

2. *Decontextualization and intentional re-creation:* The image/idea (sound/movement/word) is provisionally re-created in a medium of the artist's choice. ("I do it again, with intention.") This medium may be the same as the original, as in a word re-created into a poem, or it may be new, as in transposing an inner sensation into a painted image. In re-creation, it is removed from its original occurrence in time and space, and from its original function.

   Often the original image draws the attention of the artist because it addresses the research question metaphorically rather than literally, which is one of the distinctive qualities of art.

3. *Appreciation and discrimination:* The re-creation is assessed as to its value or the effectiveness of its expression. ("I keep it or throw it out.") Aesthetic appreciation is critical in this and the following phase. In the case of artistic inquiry, a primary concern is with how well the emerging art work addresses the research question or task. Again, in art, the question is frequently addressed metaphorically, which is only rarely (such as in physics) done in science.

4. *Refinement and transformation:* The emerging art work is manipulated, adjusted, transformed, while discriminating assessment continues in a cyclical fashion until completion. (I keep doing it until I'm satisfied.)

5. *Recontextualization:* The new creation is intentionally placed in a location appropriate to its value, which will maximize the effectiveness of its communication, and where it can be perceived, enjoyed, and assessed by self or others. ("Look here!")

This description of making art does not delve into the inner experience and dynamics of the creative process, which are addressed more fully in the chapter devoted to that aspect of artistic inquiry. My intention here is only to elucidate what I believe to be the defining behaviors of art-making. Each of these steps of art-making is present in some form whether the artistic methods are used for data collection, analysis, or presentation of findings. These steps are also consistent regardless of how modest or ambitious the work may be.

ARTISTIC METHODS OF GATHERING DATA

To reiterate, art as data is not enough. In the three hypothetical research projects described at the opening of this chapter, art works (drawings, poems, and dances) may have been made by the subjects, but not in relation or response to the research question. In other words, the art-making was not part of the research. To illustrate, if the art therapist had a research question about the experience of alcoholism or cocaine addiction, and asked her patients to make art in response to the question, then it would be artistic inquiry. If the dance therapist had asked the group to create a dance with her about the difficulty they were having and used this dance as the data with which to work, then it would be artistic inquiry. In both these revised examples, the data would have been collected using artistic methods.

Art can be made as data in response to a research question using any medium and can be created by either the researcher or the subjects/coresearchers. In artistic inquiry (one of the creative characteristics of which is an evolving method or form) the research questions may actually be formulated through the making of art, and art/data may be created in response to the questions at any time during the process.

THE DANCE/MOVEMENT THERAPY RESEARCH ATTITUDE PROJECT. In "Dance/movement therapy students' feelings and attitudes about doing research" (see Appendix), one of the ways that the students communicated their feelings to the researcher was artistic. They were asked to make spontaneous squiggle drawings reflecting their immediate feelings in response to the question of how they felt about doing research at this moment. Thus the data in this case was a collection of nonrepresentational pictures collected though artistic methods.

ARTISTIC METHODS OF DATA ANALYSIS

In all forms of research, data analysis basically makes sense of the data. It may involve much organizing and reorganizing, finding patterns, forming similar meaning units, recognizing themes. It may consist of passing the data through transformative processes, such as mathematical formulas. In artistic inquiry, the transformative processes are artistic methods, which again, in this context, means art-making. The ultimate goal is to find meaning in the data to understand what it is offering in response to the research question or to uncover its truth. Can art-making do this?

Perhaps it would be helpful to revisit the discussion about truth begun in Chapter 1. Can art-making reveal truth/meaning/understanding? Several eminent thinkers, among them, Martin Heidegger, in "The Origin of the Work of Art" (1971/1976), emphatically believed so. Heidegger explained the truth revealed in art as the artist's struggle between what he called "world" (roughly translated as the content, meaning, or idea wishing to be expressed) and "earth" (the medium or materials worked with). This struggle could be considered a kind of data analysis.

Philosopher of art R.G.Collingwood (1939) proposed that the artist has an emotional response to the stimulus/data and that the ensuing art work expresses this emotion. In the process the artist learns what the emotion is or what the meaning of the experience/object is.

John Dewey wrote that art had the quality of "clarifying and concentrating meanings contained in scattered and weakened ways in the material of other experiences" (1934/1976, p.579). He saw art as "a dynamic, self-forming, self-fulfilling, interaction between man and reality. Through . . . which an *inner meaningfulness* is progressively developed, the individual reaches a consummatory conclusion which is the building up of the *total meaning* of the experience in terms of immanent, i.e., qualitative, meaning" (emphasis added, p. 579).

It would seem then that the emergence of truth/meaning/understanding lies somewhere within the dialogue between the data and the artist/researcher. The art-making then "unconceals" (Heidegger, 1971/1976) the meaning of the data as much to the artist as to any eventual audience.

KINDS OF ARTISTIC DATA ANALYSIS. There are two kinds of data analysis that have been identified by researchers in the fields of creative arts therapy and psychology that would meet the qualifications for artistic methods and could be applied to research in dance/movement therapy.

Clark Moustakas (1990) suggested creating art work to explore, discover, synthesize, or express the meaning of the data. He described *creative synthesis* in his explication of heuristic research.

> The researcher as scientist-artist develops as aesthetic rendition of the themes and essential meanings of the phenomenon. The researcher taps into imaginative and contemplative sources of knowledge and insight in synthesizing the experience, in presenting the discovery of essences – peaks and valleys, highlights and horizons. In the creative synthesis, there is free reign of thought and feeling that supports the researcher's knowledge, passion, and presence; this infuses the work with a personal, professional, and literary value that can be expressed through a narrative, story, poem, work of art, metaphor, analogy, or tale. (1990. p. 52)

One of the kinds of artistic research that McNiff (1993, 1998) and Knill, Barba and Fuchs (1995) have proposed is *dialogue* with the images in works of art rather than interpretation based on projection or on the application of a predetermined set of corresponding meanings. (These two later types are both used in the Rorschach tests, for instance.) "*Dialogue transcripts* of the archetypal tradition...focus on the aesthetic response uttered in dialogue with the image" (Knill et al, p. 162). This dialogue between artist and image takes form verbally or through other mediums, and allows the "images to speak for themselves" (Knill et al, p. 162). McNiff has demonstrated this method as a therapeutic tool extensively in his book *Art as Medicine* (1993).

Examples of these kinds of analysis can be constructed by referring back to two of the three hypothetical examples given earlier in this chapter.

- A Jungian, psychoanalytic, expressive arts therapist examines the entire body of literature written by an eminent poet who was documented as having had a mental illness during a particular phase of his writing career. She does not develop a personality profile for the poet, but rather develops a research question about what this particular poet's archetypal imagery may offer toward understanding the relationship between artistic expression and recovery from mental illness. Being an aspiring poet herself, she writes poems that dialogue with the archetypal imagery in the original poetry. Through this method she learns more about how her own psyche is impacted by her artistic expression. She also learns more about the meaning of the archetypes she engages in the process, and develops a theory about how they might behave in the psyche of other people suffering and recovering from mental illness. She then amplifies her research by asking other therapists with artistic abilities to dialogue with these same archetypal images through artistic expression in other mediums.

- To develop greater insight into ongoing difficulties she is experiencing in a particular group, a dance/movement therapist does a complete Kestenberg Movement Profile on herself and the group. She uses a video tape of a previously recorded, especially problematic dance/movement therapy session as her data. She sees a clash in movement qualities between herself and a very active male group member. Without further interpretation, she shows what she has found to the group and to reach a deeper understanding of it, she invites the man to join her in creating a dance that explores the dynamics of the clash. The other group members serve as witnesses who can then provide feedback about the dance. The group as a whole then discusses the implications of the dance for the dynamics of their group process.

THE DANCE/MOVEMENT THERAPY RESEARCH ATTITUDE PROJECT. While pointing out the artistic methods of data analysis that occurred in "Dance/movement therapy student's attitudes about doing research" (see Appendix) I will also be referring back to an earlier section of this chapter, "Actions that result in art." Hopefully this will serve to further illustrate the actions described and clarify how they are artistic methods.

To analyze the pictorial data artistically, the whole class began by looking at all the pictures held up by participants in front of them while seated together in a circle. After silently looking at all the pictures for awhile, participants were asked to identify and describe how other pictures reminded them of their own. This led to a general discussion about the various qualities of the line drawings: use of space, line intensity, direction of movement, shape, etc. After building this descriptive vocabulary together, participants were asked to move around the space and form small groups with those whose pictures "belonged together" because of their common qualities. The only criterion for belonging to a small group was that all of its members had to agree that all the pictures belonged there. Thus small groups were formed that contained pictures with common visual themes that had been analyzed aesthetically by the participants themselves, thereby avoiding any external interpretive analysis.

If the analysis had ended here, no artistic methods would have occurred beyond the data collection. It had been analyzed from an aesthetic perspective by the artists themselves but had not involved art-making as part of the analysis. However, because of how the analysis proceeded next, the work done thus far can be understood as the *initial awareness* stage of art-making. The artists/researchers were increasing their alertness to images that drew their attention, in this case because of their similarities to one another.

The work done in the small clusters moved the art-making on to *decontextualization* and *intentional re-creation*. Each group was asked to make a small dance that for them captured the aesthetic qualities of their collective pictures. To do this, the images from the drawings were essentially removed from their original context and re-created as movements by cluster members. Through cooperative *appreciation* and *discrimination*, movement suggestions were selected or rejected by the group. The movements were then *refined* and *transformed* into completed dances.

All analysis was done within the process of art-making as defined earlier in this chapter. Meaning was revealed through purely artistic and aesthetic means. Words were not used to describe the meanings of the drawings, but the aesthetic qualities that were explicitly identified and implicitly communicated spoke volumes as to the feelings and attitudes of the artists/co-researchers.

ARTISTIC METHODS OF PRESENTING FINDINGS

Presenting findings, in artistic inquiry, refers to creating the finished presentational form in which the findings will be communicated, as well as performing or displaying it to an audience in that form. Even if no other aspect of the research was artistic, the findings could possibly still be given artistic form and presented artistically as such. As Elliott Eisner suggested: "The mind draws upon a variety of forms of knowing to give birth to ideas, and these ideas, I am arguing, need not be expressed in the modes within which the conceptualization has occurred" (1985a, p. 127). An example of research that used this approach will be given at the conclusion of this chapter (Glesne, 1997).

In traditional research, the medium is meant to disappear as it reveals meaning. The researcher works to make the words, numbers, or graphs transparent, even as they are finely crafted. It does not add to the meaning of the research if our attention is drawn to how well the words sit on the page or how boldly expressive the bars on the graph are. If the researcher does attend to the aesthetics of words or line, it is always in the service of drawing attention away from them by more efficiently communicating the meaning of the findings. As a rule, if the visuals are too flashy or the words too creative, it is viewed as an unnecessary distraction from the findings.

This use of word, line and number is akin to what Heidegger (1971/1976) described as craft. The medium is "used up" in the making, the way wood is used up to build a house. The wood is still there, but the revealing of its woodness is not the purpose of the house. His description of art is distinctly different. In the art work, the medium is meant to "shine forth" its essence as it conveys meaning. The artist's task is to allow the medium to express both itself and whatever meaning is also being revealed through it.

In contrast to how wood is used up in craft, Heidegger described the art of painting: "To be sure, the painter also uses pigment, but in such a way that color is not used up but rather only now comes to shine forth" (1971/1976, p. 675). Because "color shines and wants only to shine" (p. 674), the artist must wrestle with it (or any medium) to keep it from consuming the meaning that also needs to come forth through the art work.

I don't believe there is necessarily a clear-cut distinction between craft and art and imagine instead a continuum between the two ideas. Works that are more like craft are more functional than aesthetic, and works that are more like art are more aesthetic, thereby more concerned with the shining forth of the medium *and* the message than with the function. Certainly there are many fine works that straddle art and craft by being both functional and aesthetic. A question relevant to this discussion then is "Where along this continuum does artistic inquiry lie?" Perhaps because it attempts to be functional as well as aesthetic, it falls somewhere between craft and art. (Because the medium is meant to disappear in service of the function in traditional research, could it be considered more like a craft?) In making and displaying a work of art as the final form in which the findings of research are communicated, the medium and the message are both revealed, but the beauty or appearance of the medium must not be allowed to outshine the message.

The final step of art-making is *recontextualization,* or the placing of the art work in a context appropriate to its value, where its meaning may be best revealed. Heidegger called this "*Preserving the work...*a sober standing-within the extraordinary awesomeness of the truth that is happening in the work" (emphasis added, 1971/1976, p. 691). It is clear from his writing that the preservation is as essential to the expression of artistic truth as is any part of the art-making process. After all, if the value of the art work is not recognized, or if it is improperly placed in the world, it will have no opportunity to reveal truth. In terms of research, how the findings are displayed, and in what context will determine its ability to communicate.

An example of this can be constructed from one of the initial hypothetical research projects:

- Over a period of several years, an art therapist collects the drawings of all the in patients in a program for early recovery from alcoholism and cocaine addiction. He selects the art works that most powerfully express the experiences of those who made them. He mounts or frames them, divides them into two groups by whether the artists were alcoholics or cocaine addicts and creates an exhibit that accentuates the aesthetic differences between the two groups. He displays aesthetic commentary alongside the art works to increase the observers' ability to perceive these differences. In addition he creates an accompanying pamphlet that offers his understanding of these differences based on a more psychological interpretation of the data for those who are interested. To this exhibit he invites fellow art therapists, as well as those who have influence (i.e., administrators, insurance company representatives, board members) in deciding whether the existing treatment program should be changed to adapt to the differing needs of what he sees as two distinct populations.

THE DANCE/MOVEMENT THERAPY RESEARCH ATTITUDE PROJECT. The dances that expressed the aesthetic qualities of each small cluster's drawings were performed for the whole class. In response to each dance, the audience described its aesthetic qualities. This reflection process not only allowed the artists to see their pictures/dances in new ways, but it gave all participants a fuller understanding of the meaning that was expressed in both their own and others' dances. Thus understanding proceeded to deeper levels without the aid of interpretation from a psychological or scientific theoretical perspective.

The presentations creatively communicated not the negative-positive continuum of feelings (as did the numbers from one to ten), but the subtle and complex, three-dimensional, embodied, visceral truths of the participants' responses to research. The dances were not as cognitively explicit as were the narratives that followed, but they succinctly conveyed an essence that the viewers were able to intuitively identify.

This recontextualization or preservation of the work, as Heidegger would call it, was appropriate to the purpose of the research and maximized the value of the art works that were created for that purpose. This was the audience to whom the dances would be the most meaningful and who would be most able to see the truths revealed.

THREE EXAMPLES OF ARTISTIC METHODS OF INQUIRY

PHOTOGRAPHING THE SELF. Robert Ziller (1990) conducted psycho/sociological research on "self theory" using photographs taken by subjects in response to questions such as "'Who are you?" "What does the good life mean to you?" "What does woman mean?" "What does war mean?" "What does the United States mean to you?" (p. 10). Although the data were photographs, Ziller does not refer to them as art and nowhere does he attempt to assess their aesthetic qualities. This research is squarely located within the social science tradition, even though it uses visual data exclusively and breaks the tradition of the researcher as the observer/photographer.

However, in his introduction, Ziller briefly states "Through photography we instantly become artists, " (p. 37) and in this statement implicitly acknowledges an artistic method used by his subjects to gather data. Therefore, it is just barely possible to consider this artistic inquiry, although this is the first and last reference he makes to art-making.

This example suggests possibilities for artistic methods of gathering data in dance/movement therapy research. Could coresearchers be given cameras and asked to respond to questions similar to Ziller's and then treat the photographs as works of art or stimuli for dances that would deepen the exploration of the questions? Could coresearchers photograph one another while moving/dancing/responding to the research questions? One of the challenges we face in dance/movement therapy is the temporal nature of our primary medium. How might photographs be used to artistically document data collection, analysis, and presentation; to preserve the work?

"THAT RARE FEELING: RE-PRESENTING RESEARCH THROUGH POETIC TRANSCRIPTION." Educational researcher Corrine Glesne (1997) interviewed an elderly Puerto Rican professor of education, on site at the University of Puerto Rico, about her life work. She analyzed the transcribed ten hours of audio-tapes using qualitative methods that included thematic coding and sorting of the data. At that point Glesne chose to divert significantly from the condoned qualitative methods to what she termed *poetic transcription*, which she defined as "the creation of poemlike compositions from the words of interviewees" (p. 202). She compared the qualitative methods with which she was more familiar to this experimental method that evolved during this analysis:

> Analytical writing breaks up interview transcriptions and observation field notes into component parts, imposing a researcher-perceived order on things. . . . Poetic transcription is also filtered through the researcher but involves word reduction while illuminating the wholeness and interconnections of thoughts. Instead of piecing together aspects of Dona Juana's story into a chronological representational puzzle of her life (with pieces missing), I found myself, through poetic transcription, searching for the essence conveyed, the hues, the textures, and then drawing from all the portions of the interviews to juxtapose details into a somewhat abstract re-presentation. (Glesne, 1997, p. 206)

The results were six poetic transcriptions that used only the words of her interviewee "shaped by [the] researcher to give pleasure and truth" (1997, p. 213). Glesne distinguished between Truth with a capital "T" that is conveyed in poetry, and truth of the sort conveyed in poetic transcriptions, which she said "approaches poetry" in form and intent (p. 213). She called this the "truth of description, re-presenting a perspective or experience of the interviewee, filtered through the researcher" (p. 213).

Regardless of whether the transcriptions can be considered poetry or poetic, the methods of art-making were present both in her data analysis and in the presentation of findings. Glesne's research provides inspiration for the use of what could be called "dance transcription" in dance/movement therapy research. Imagine gathering the dances of a client, (who could be a collaborator addressing the research question) on videotape, like a transcript. While viewing them repeatedly, gestures and phrases could be selected that spoke most clearly to the research question, or the living experience of the client. The researcher/artist/clinician could then create a dance that, like Glesne's poems did for Dona Juana's story, might attempt to "illuminate her truth" (1997, p. 215). Although the dance could not be published (recontextualized) in a journal as Glesne's work was, it could be presented at a conference of researchers interested in similar methods of inquiry or clinicians working with people like the one whose story inspired the dance. In the next chapter, an example of a similar artistic inquiry will be considered in depth.

THE LIVING PSYCHE. Edward Edinger, a Jungian analyst, attempted "to demonstrate graphically the reality of the living psyche" (1990, p. xiii) by publishing selected art works and journal entries created by a patient during five years of a ten-year psycho analysis. Little is said by Edinger of the process of the methodology or any aspect of the coresearcher relationship so there is no way to tell how the journal and art samples were selected.

What makes this research valuable to the discussion of artistic inquiry is not that Edinger's data was art, but that he aesthetically preserved and presented 104 artworks with a willingness to allow them and their creator to communicate meaning directly to the reader/audience. Across from every full page devoted to a painting, Edinger included a description by the patient, and an interpretation by the analyst (himself) from a clearly stated archetypal perspective. The effect is very much like a commemorative publication of a museum or gallery art exhibit. Although Edinger's interpretations could be viewed as reductionistic, the value of this research lies in the respect shown for what is communicated by the art works themselves. This allows the viewers to do their own analysis and draw their own conclusions.

Like Ziller's research, the qualification of *The living psyche* as artistic inquiry is not strong, but points to a method that could be used in dance/movement therapy. Could the dances of patients, preserved and presented as works of art with minimal interpretation, further understanding of the therapeutic process?

SUMMARY

The distinguishing characteristic of artistic inquiry that this chapter addresses is the use of actions that result in art, or art-making as data collection, analysis, or presentation. It was pointed out that art as data is not sufficient in and of itself to qualify research as artistic. It was also clarified that interpretation of art that does not involve art-making as part of the analysis is not sufficient to be considered artistic inquiry.

The art-making process was described in five stages to clarify what kinds of actions might be considered artistic methods.

1. Initial awareness
2. Decontextualization and intentional re-creation
3. Appreciation and discrimination
4. Refinement and transformation
5. Recontextualization

Three hypothetical and four actual examples of research that used art-making as data collection, data analysis, or data presentation were provided for illustration.

In the following chapter, similarities may be seen between the characteristics of art-making and the phases of the creative process. The difference between the foci of the two chapters is that this one sought to clarify the nature of art-making behavior in particular, while the next will attempt to delve more deeply into some of the internal processes of more generic creativity.

Chapter 4

INQUIRY THAT ACKNOWLEDGES A
CREATIVE PROCESS

INTRODUCTION

EMINENT SCIENTISTS AND PHILOSOPHERS have pointed out similarities between creativity in science and art (Beveridge, 1950; Bohm & Peat, 1987; Bronowski, 1981; Capra, 1982; Einstein, 1945; Griffin, 1988; Kuhn, 1970; Panek, 1999; Poincare, 1908; Schaffer, 1994), and often I have used these similarities to support the validity of a more creative approach to research. In fact, in considering inquiry that engages in a creative process, I am challenged to imagine what a non-creative approach to research might be! A necessary effort to this discussion, however, is to clarify what creative process is and to distinguish research processes that engage in and acknowledge it from those that do not. Shaun McNiff offered one example of what creative research is not:

> If experimentation is to correspond to the spontaneous and complex movements of art and the therapeutic process, *it cannot be planned and controlled.* We can observe patterns, repetitions and similarities but the conditions of art and psychotherapy *are not subject to experimental replication.* (emphasis added, 1993, p. 4)

Another, and perhaps more critical, point that must be made is the importance of *acknowledging* a creative process in the research. As the writers to which I referred above have pointed out, there is creativity involved in much scientific research, but it is very rarely reported as intrinsic or valuable to method. Artistic inquiry would correct this omission by including in its methodology a descriptive acknowledgment of the creative aspects of the research process.

After discussing creative process as it relates to artistic inquiry, I will again turn to "Identifying dance/movement therapy students' feelings and attitudes about doing research" (see Appendix) and an article by Patricia Fenner (1996) describing her heuristic research project in art therapy to illustrate this aspect of artistic inquiry.

CREATIVE PROCESS

To create involves the emergence of idea into consciousness and the manifestation of that idea into communicable form. Creativity is the cluster of qualities or abilities needed to create. One popular theory divides creativity conceptually into *process, product, press,* and *person* (Mooney, 1963). In research, methodology can be compared to process, which in creativity refers to dynamic movement toward some purpose or product and can range from visibly active to quietly internal, as it is in thought. The product, in the case of research, would be the presentation of findings; a culmination that has traditionally had a final and unchanging form. Press refers to the environment and how it impacts the creative or research effort. Person refers to those who design and carry out the research. In this chapter, the focus will be primarily on process and on the characteristics of the creative person as they reflect those of many dance/movement therapists.

EMERGENT AND INNOVATIVE METHODS. The scientific method uses established research methods to discover new information. But art is as much, if not more, about new innovative methods as it is about new information. Through the creative process, the artistic researcher discovers new ways of doing research in hopes of finding new meaning in subjects that may have been previously examined by old methods. A creative research process is one that does not follow a proscribed method but evolves from a consciousness changed by emerging information. The artist/researcher feels the pull of opposing tensions, such as old versus new contradictory data, which through a creative synthesis are resolved into a new form.

Creative process is often conceptualized as moving through phases, each with a different dynamic, purpose, and feeling for the creator. The process, as I envision it, has six phases (modified from many other creativity theories) that may recur cyclically: inception, perception, inner dialogue, illumination, expression/formation, and outer dialogue. Not all creativity theorists, and certainly not all researchers or artists, will conceptualize creative process the way I have here. However, inquirers who I would deem artistic will somehow acknowledge a respect for and understanding of the unprogrammed ways they have proceeded through experiences similar to these.

INCEPTION. Compelling curiosity or disturbance about an idea marks its dawning. Out of this experience, eventually a question will take form. The question is rarely articulated at the outset but rather may be only a new awareness of, for instance, an image, melody, phrase, or movement; or a vague discomfort that leads to restlessness and exploratory activity in a particular medium. Although the question may not become explicit until later in the creative process, for research it realistically may need to be stated before a research proposal or grant application can be completed.

PERCEPTION. In this phase, the artist/researcher actively seeks stimuli from external sources that satisfy her or his curiosity about the question. In dance and choreography, this phase can consist of extended improvisation and may involve watching other dancers work on the same theme and drawing movement ideas from them. A dance/movement therapist doing artistic inquiry might in this phase view videotapes of a particular client, then move along with the video until the therapist reaches visual and kinesthetic saturation with the movement. In all cases, the artist/researcher is immersed in the desired stimuli.

This phase is equivalent to gathering data, but in artistic inquiry is distinguished by perceptual openness and a kind of relational dialogue with the sensory data during which the consciousness of the artist/researcher is changed by the perceptions. This change may be very gradual, as so much information is absorbed indirectly and stored as tacit knowledge, only to rise to consciousness when it can no longer be ignored.

Perception has many different styles. Stimuli can be taken in passively or actively. It can be pursued with what may seem like self-destructive intent, (literally or metaphorically) order for old ego-syn-

UNIVERSITY OF HERTFORDSHIRE LRC

tonic concepts to be destroyed so that new ones can take their place. Artist/researchers may experience themselves as devouring the data, breaking it down, and assimilating it in preparation for the inner dialogue. Perception can be colored by an infinite variety of unique skills, which Eisner referred to in *The Enlightened Eye* (1991) as determining connoisseurship in various fields. Different kinds of training enable the perception of different qualities, forms, and essential meanings in the data.

INNER DIALOGUE. Comparable to data analysis, the inner dialogue is a process of making sense of the stimuli in which one has been immersed. It involves symbolically digesting all that has been swallowed or cooking everything that has gone into the pot. In traditional scientific research, the process is primarily a controlled, cognitive, and conscious one during which predetermined methods are applied to carefully organized and coded data. In artistic inquiry, the sensory data may not be so clearly organized and may in fact be stored only in the consciousness (or even the unconscious) of the artist. What makes the inner dialogue with the data creative is not knowing how it will proceed or how the data will change the artist/researcher and the research question during the process.

If we return to the example of the dance/movement therapist whose data are videotaped images of a client, she might at this point analyze or seek to understand the movement by using any number of methods. She could apply a systematic and standardized analysis tool like Labananalysis or the Kestenberg Movement Profile, which would be much like scientific research. In contrast, one of the most frequently used methods that dance therapists use to make meaning of movement is to move with the client and through attunement and kinesthetic empathy gain understanding of the feelings and experiences of the client. When encountering the client's movement in this intimate manner, the dance/therapist does not know how she will be impacted, but trusts that she will be able to respond empathically and creatively. Alternatively, she could view the movement through the aesthetic values of the profession, noting its authenticity, the story it tells, the depth and articulation of emotional expression, its use of space and time, and so forth. Perhaps most creatively, she could improvise on the themes that emerged while she moved along with the videotapes and develop her own unique dance response to them. Whereas in most research the data analysis is expected to be replicable by any other researcher, in artistic inquiry it is assumed that the process is unique to each particular artist/researcher.

I refer to this phase as an inner dialogue because all the parts of the artist/researcher are, in a way, conversing: the body, intellect, emotions, intuitions, and spirit are working together. The creative process may be partially unconscious, allowing patterns and meanings to emerge in their own time and in surprisingly serendipitous ways. The artist/researcher may also be open to transpersonal meaning revealed from sources beyond him or herself.

ILLUMINATION. More a moment than a phase, illumination is most apt to occur during times of relaxed surrender of ego-driven action. Although frequently experienced after laborious attention to and saturation with the data, it may also come as inspiration at any point during the creative process. The term illumination has been used by most creativity theorists because it describes the frequently identified experience of the light (knowledge, truth, awareness, heightened consciousness) suddenly shining in the darkness. It is the most easily recognized moment of emergence of idea into the consciousness of the artist/researcher.

Idea is often illumined symbolically. In these cases, the insight that appears to the intuitive researcher may be in the form of a metaphor for a solution or a missing piece of the puzzle. Frequently, the metaphorical image is a synthesis or integration of components of the data previously seen as polarized.

EXPRESSION/FORMATION. Although sometimes answers to the questions arrive like revelations, at other times the sense of order or resolution emerges slowly and with persistent, conscious effort. When a sense of meaning is finally discerned amidst the chaos, the artist/researcher's purpose turns toward expressing it in some communicable form. Again, in scientific research the form is often predetermined, and the researcher basically fills in the findings and follows a report format acceptable to the scientific publications. In artistic inquiry, the findings can essentially take any form that the artist/researcher sees as effective, including metaphorical. This makes understanding of the final form challenging for those who are more accustomed to literal or representational meaning.

Our dance/movement therapist with her videotapes might at this point create a dance that expresses her understanding of the essence of the client's movement or her own response to it as the therapist.

The form is determined by and inseparable from the content or the meaning needing to be conveyed. The inquiring artist must select one from the infinite options available that will best manifest the desired qualities. His or her abilities and resources, as well as the venue within which it will be presented, will in part determine this.

Expression/formation is the phase most often associated with the creative, artistic process, as its products are often the only part shared with others. It is also the most challenging and rewarding phase. The process of giving form to an idea can feel like a struggle to make the data (and the chosen medium) take a form that the artist/researcher knows will have the qualities that reflect its essential meaning. But when the struggle is over, the result is not only a transformation of the data and the medium, but of the artist/researcher as well.

No matter how the findings take form, it is still the researcher's responsibility to present the findings as meaningful in relation to the motivating question. The artistic inquirer must also answer the final questions, "So what?" and, "Who cares?" by connecting the findings to the context within which the research question arose. This recontextualization needs to happen in this and the following phase.

OUTER DIALOGUE. The ultimate purpose of research, and art, is to communicate a new vision or understanding of a phenomenon. So, once this vision is given form, the product is then placed in an environment within which it can be intentionally perceived by others. In traditional research, the environment or context is very often a professionally juried publication or conference. The work is evaluated, accepted or rejected, and then receives collegial or editorial feedback from the larger community of professional peers and mentors to the researcher. If well received, the findings may by applied back into the matrix from which the research emerged and may create immediate change. This feedback and potential impact is the function of the outer dialogue.

In artistic inquiry, the outer dialogue may proceed similarly. The venue of presentation could be a gallery, theater, literary publication or the world wide web, and the evaluation might come in the form of a critique of the aesthetic value of the work rather than its practical applicability. The value of the inquiry might be assessed by completely different criteria, such as the aesthetic values identified in the previous chapter. Feedback might be sought as to whether the work inspired new insights in its viewers.

In the case of our dance/movement therapist's creative case study, change might result from sharing her vision with colleagues through a dance performance at a professional conference. If the dance is effective and touches the audience, her colleagues might apply to their work deeper understandings of the experiences of the client and therapist portrayed.

THE CREATIVE RESEARCHER

As in any kind of research, so much of the process depends on the skills and training of the researcher. In the case of artistic inquiry, there are particular abilities or personality traits that facilitate a creative process. Shaun McNiff summarized scientific philosopher W.I.B. Beveridge's description of the necessary characteristics of creative scientists that have parallels in artists. These are all skills that are also necessary to the practice of dance/movement therapy, and so dance/movement therapists can apply them to the practice of artistic inquiry as well:

> The need to explore the widest range of possibilities and chance events; imagination; openness; persistence; the ability to change strategies in response to the material under review; the mixing of disciplines; a willingness to err; intuition; an interest in the unknown; an inability to simply follow the tradition of logical analysis; personal powers of observation and interpretation. (McNiff, 1986, p. 282)

Of all these abilities, I don't think that imagination and intuition can be overemphasized as necessary to the creative process. Together they open consciousness to the infinite possibilities that may present themselves during the artistic research endeavor. Without them inquiry can only be uninspired and mechanical.

Social scientist Judi Marshall (1981), when interviewed by fellow qualitative researchers, described her data analysis process. Clearly it parallels the kind of creative process that has been described by many artists, scientists, psychologists, and educators. Embedded in her informal yet articulate description are at least the following six intimations of the strengths that make her the kind of researcher she is and why her work can be described as creative. It is not difficult to imagine dance/movement therapists, who are so experienced with creative process, having similar responses if they, for example, used

dance/movement as data, improvisation as data analysis, and choreography as presentation.

- *Researcher/self as medium.* Marshall began with the statement:
  "My job as a researcher is to be an open and receptive
  medium through which this order comes out" (1981, p. 395).
  Being the medium requires trust in one's self as the "ultimate translator" (p. 399). It necessitates viewing oneself
  with an ability to recognize rightness of feeling and knowing while interpreting the data.

- *Taking risks and entering into the unknown.* Of one phase in her
  process Marshall said, "So at this point there is an excitement that something *is* coming out of the data, but if anyone
  asks me I have no idea what, and will avoid being forced
  into saying! And at the same time there's a fear that *nothing*
  is going to come out of the research" (p. 396). Approaching
  the unknown with confidence requires courage, faith and an
  adventurous spirit.

- *Tolerating anxiety about chaos and meaninglessness.* Regarding
  the almost unbearably gradual emergence of meaning from
  the data, Marshall hypothesized, "I think this is partly about
  how much anxiety and uncertainty you're willing to tolerate
  for how long; I think the more you can, the better the analysis will work out" (p. 397). In this she implicitly warns
  against premature resolution of ambiguity.

- *Rigor.* Near the end of the process Marshall described how
  the challenges intensified. "Things start to get tough, as if
  I'm holding all this stuff in my head and beginning to feel
  overloaded. I need then to close, I'm getting tired, I want
  to bring things together and capture it all, it feels as if I
  won't be able to hold onto it much longer" (p. 398). There
  are several phases in creative process that are highly stress-
  ful for the very reasons Marshall experienced and require
  rigorous intentionality and commitment to the process.

- *Surrender to immersion.* Her work required her full involvement on many levels. She described it as all-consuming and
  difficult to do in small doses. It was difficult to break

through inertia, give up distractions and immerse herself fully in it, and then difficult to get out of it and back to other aspects of her life again. She described it as being a "whole-mind activity" (p. 397). Marshall also recognized the importance of letting go of unnecessary data, schematic diagrams that didn't work, and out-moded conceptualizations in service of the analysis. Her description suggests a surrender to complete saturation, to the flow of uncontrolled events, and a surrendering of concepts that the ego may be tempted to grasp onto in the interest of its own perpetuation.

- *Open to unconscious material through inspiration.* (In this context, "unconscious" is used to mean information that is not within the awareness of the researcher at a given time.) Like others who are open to creative process, Marshall received "flashes of inspiration which often turn out to be quite important." When her analysis started to come together, "insights start to come from some sort of unconscious level.... I really have some kind of 'broad band' attention when lots of things seem to be connecting, when I can see over horizons in all sorts of directions. Lots of things come into my consciousness which perhaps I hadn't been aware of for years, and my mind is able to make connection at all sorts of levels" (p. 397). To receive inspiration one must be in a state of openness to information "coming into consciousness" from sources not always recognized as self. This information may at times seem strange, contradictory and uncomfortable, and needs to be accepted by the researcher without premature judgment until its value has been considered with what the Buddhists call an "unsaturated" mind.

Some skills that dance/movement therapists have, in addition to those identified by McNiff and Marshall, that are so uniquely suited to creative research process include flexibility, spontaneity, ease of self-expression in chosen medium(s), playfulness, emotional accessibility, faith in the creative process, tolerance of ambiguity, the ability to work without controlling the variables, and the ability to discern patterns in unorganized data.

CREATIVE PROCESS IN "IDENTIFYING DANCE/MOVEMENT THERAPY STUDENTS' FEELINGS ATTITUDES ABOUT DOING RESEARCH"

Referring back to the characteristics of creative process identified earlier in this chapter, it is evident that this small research project (see Appendix) engaged a creative process in several ways even in a short amount of time. Additionally, what is not mentioned in the description of the project is that the methodology creatively evolved over a period of years while doing versions of this research with many students in several different fields. Each time I introduced the artistic portion to a group, I tweaked and tuned it to meet the needs of the moment and to improve my facilitation of their creative data analysis. Adjustment and adaptation, requiring flexibility, occurred in this instance when some students couldn't find a small cluster of similar drawings to join. I find myself communicating differently to each group of students depending on what I know of their learning styles and their mood in the moment. Because I am not attempting to control or categorize their responses, but rather encourage their creativity, these improvisations on my part are not only necessary but also helpful to the process.

As the primary researcher, during the collection of the drawing data and the subsequent clustering and creation of dances that reflected the drawings' aesthetic qualities, I basically created a fertile situation in which to surrender the data analysis to the creativity of my coresearchers. This required faith in their creative processes: in their ability to discern patterns in chaos, and to create dances with almost no direction on my part. They literally became the medium as they explored expressive movement with their own bodies. I had to allow a flow of uncontrolled events that eventually resulted in the creation and understanding of meaningful works of art. Like Marshall, my coresearchers and I entered into the research not knowing how it would proceed or how it would change our feelings, attitudes, and perceptions. It is evident that it did alter the feelings of some of the coresearchers as they remarked on their changed perspective during the transition from the drawing/dancing to the textual data analysis.

After our research procedures were completed, we entered the outer dialogue together by talking over our experience of the research and our impressions of the results. Their feedback about the process and the product influenced my further development of the project. Incorporating the written report into this document invites further outer dialogue and possibility for refinement. Eventually the report may be submitted to a professional journal where it will receive further critical feedback. My peers and colleagues will then determine its value and meaning to others.

CREATIVE PROCESS IN "HEURISTIC RESEARCH STUDY: SELF-THERAPY USING THE BRIEF IMAGE-MAKING EXPERIENCE"

In 1996, *The Arts in Psychotherapy* journal published this unusual article by Patricia Fenner, an art therapist from Australia, describing a project in which she was both researcher and subject. Her study investigated "an approach that uses the brief drawing experience of five minutes over approximately a two-month period in order to determine its value to enhancement of personal meaning and therapeutic change" (p. 37). In her words, it fell "outside the bounds of conventional research methodology" (p. 37). To meet the needs of her "emergent" (p. 37) data gathering and analysis design, Fenner modified the heuristic research model, which has been richly explicated by Clark Moustakas (1990). She identified aspects of immersion, incubation, illumination, and explication (without Moustakas' initial engagement and final creative synthesis) in her methodology. Although she never identified her work as being creative per se, the processes she describes at length clearly parallel those identified by Moustakas as intrinsically creative.

Briefly, her methodology began by creating a five-minute drawing every day at the same time and under the same conditions, that reflected her state of being at that moment. She then responded verbally to each drawing and concluded with a second drawing. For two months she collected these drawings as well as transcriptions of her audiotaped verbal responses. She then entered into an extensive, in-depth dialogue with the entire collection in several stages that she described in detail. During this time she suspended all presuppositions and references to psychological theory "in order to achieve a direct contact with the phenomenon of my experiencing" (1996, p. 37). Themes emerged from "the dense, unordered, chaotic experience" (p. 37) and were distilled, reflecting what she felt was the phenomenological meaning of her drawings.

Fenner described this entire analysis as evolving. "Each step has followed its predecessor in order to organically approach the experience of self from an always fresh and more focused perspective" (1996, p. 41). This analysis was not predetermined. "In fact, I did not know what step or process might follow [the] initial exercise [the first drawings and responses], though experience led me to the hunch that something of interest [might] arise" (p. 39). She quoted Michael Polanyi as defining hunches such as these as intuition or "the conviction that there is something there to be discovered" (p. 39). It is obvious that trusting her hunches or her intuition was active in many of the following aspects of creative process that Fenner described in her methodology.

She described an attitude of openness to her data and its emergent meaning during the analysis that reflected trust of self as the medium of analysis. "I am both the phenomenon and the researcher" (1996, p. 41). Her words also indicate surrender to complete immersion in what she, like Moustakas, called indwelling: "I was living and breathing my investigation. In spite of a commitment to separating from my indwelling experiences in break periods, the intensity of the personal meanings...overwhelmed rational obligation" (p. 41). This and the following excerpt reflect conditions in which unconscious material becomes available for illumination: "It would seem that the activation of the tacit realm during a period of incubation was ready to provide me with meaningful insights" (p. 41). She described these insights as resulting in "new self-knowledge and experiential change at the bodily level" as well as an "enhanced sense of well-being" (p. 51), providing evidence of being transformed by the creative research process.

The attention that Fenner gave to the emerging, yet rigorous methodology was equal to that given to the emerging meaning. This was true even down to writing the journal article, which she describes as being "as much in process as about the practices that had taken place over the months of research" (1996, p. 37). It is this commitment to process and explication of method that distinguishes this research from art or from self-exploration. Yet it is the creativity intrinsic in every phase of the process that distinguishes this example of artistic inquiry from traditional scientific research.

SUMMARY

Although the last example of artistic inquiry given in this chapter was in the field of art therapy, it is not hard to imagine how a similar heuristic study could be undertaken in dance/movement therapy, with very little adaptation needed. The data could easily have been two months worth of video-taped movement for five minutes with verbal reflection. All the videotapes could then have been viewed and "moved with," and emerging movement themes identified. Just as Fenner offered to art therapy, a method of self-analysis through brief movement could be similarly developed, validated, and published as a result of rigorous creative examination by a dance/movement therapist.

Artistic inquiry acknowledges the aspects of its methodology that are creative, innovative or, as Fenner called them, emergent. The artist/researcher also needs to have certain abilities that enable successful engagement in creative experiences. Artistic inquirers are able to identify, surrender to or facilitate, and acknowledge experiences similar to those identified in phases such as inception, perception, inner dialogue, illumination, expression/formation, or outer dialogue. The artist/researcher often serves as the medium of perception, analysis, expression, and may experience being changed by the process. The research question may also be transformed as a result of emerging clarity. The purpose of artistic inquiry is not to create the findings, but to create a form that is able to reveal and express the essential qualities of the findings. But whatever form the research takes, the process is likely to be considered as important as the product or the findings.

Chapter 5

INQUIRY THAT IS AESTHETICALLY MOTIVATED AND DETERMINED

INTRODUCTION

THE TERM "AESTHETICS" HAS unfortunately been misunderstood by many to refer to someone else's rules about the determination of beauty, and "someone else" is usually an elite member of the era's dominant culture. This understanding has alienated many, especially in the postmodern era, from the study of aesthetics. However, even if we stay with the idea of beauty, we can understand aesthetics as referring to *anyone's* definition and determination of beauty. Each culture, each group, even each one of us, has our own aesthetic. We can discover our aesthetic by looking at what we consider beautiful.

If we need to move away from the idea of beauty, because of its elitist or restrictive connotations, aesthetics can be understood as *the discriminating appreciation of qualities reflected in form.* This definition presents three essential concepts: *qualities, form,* and *appreciation,* each of which is crucial to an understanding of the relevance of aesthetics to artistic inquiry.

QUALITIES. More than simply the surface characteristics or features of a thing, qualities are the perceivable manifestations of the essential nature of it.

FORM. The unique configuration of the qualities of a thing determines its form. How its qualities are arranged in space and time in relation to each other make the form exist.

APPRECIATION. The ability to perceive and respond aesthetically is in part natural and universal, as in the appreciation of the forms created by harmonious flow in nature. However, we come to appreciate many things only by repeated exposure, by examining them carefully, by knowing them well. This develops our sensibilities about that thing, and we become highly attuned to it; able to recognize its qualities quickly and easily. This kind of more specialized aesthetic sense is often developed through intentional training in the values of a particular culture. Members of that culture are then communally sensitive to and appreciative of certain qualities of form and in turn desire and encourage them.

In the discussion that follows I will focus on those particular aesthetic appreciations or values that develop through professional training in dance/movement therapy. For instance, the qualities that dance/movement therapists appreciate are reflected in the forms made by an expressive moving body. This expressive movement becomes dance through a deliberate act of consciousness that engages the aesthetic values of the creators and observers.

When I describe artistic inquiry as *aesthetically motivated,* I refer to the researcher's desire to participate in the aesthetic aspects of forming. Inquiry that is *aesthetically determined* reflects a series of discriminating choices made by the researcher in regard to the form the inquiry takes. This approach to research contrasts those in which the form is predetermined by scientifically or academically mandated procedures. In these more traditional methods, as Elliot Eisner has pointed out (1981), the *message* of the findings is the same regardless of the form that is used. In artistic inquiry, each form is selected or created specifically to communicate the meaning of particular findings and is inseparable from that meaning.

In this discussion of artistic inquiry I invite creators, consumers, and critics of research to approach the qualities of research aesthetically. I propose that as artistic researchers we need to be conscious of our aesthetic goals. As critical consumers, it is essential that we be aware of the qualities we appreciate in research, regardless of the medium in which they are expressed. If the research takes the form of dance, then our aesthetic values about dance and about research have the opportunity to either conflict or synthesize. My purpose in this discussion is to identify research that authentically represents dance/movement therapy. Therefore, after describing aesthetic consciousness, I will propose what I understand to be some of the aesthetic values of dance/movement therapy and will explore how these might interface with artistic inquiry. Examples of aesthetic motivation and determination will be given from "Identifying student attitudes and feelings about doing research," (Appendix) and "Researcher as artist/Artist as researcher" (Finley & Knowles, 1995).

AESTHETIC CONSCIOUSNESS

By aesthetic consciousness I mean a particular kind of awareness and understanding that I see as having four significant features. The first is a well-developed awareness of sensation, emotion and intuition. The second is a strong appreciation of qualities and form. The third is the ability to move between dynamically opposed perceptual and conceptual modes in rapid alternation or to work in them simultaneously. The fourth is an awareness of one's own aesthetic values.

SENSATION, EMOTION AND INTUITION. The study of aesthetics, as a branch of philosophy and a practical component of art appreciation and creation, primarily seeks to understand a distinctly human response to sensory experience. It is not about logical or abstract thought, but about sensory comprehension of the material world and the consequent responses like repulsion or desire, calm or excitement. In addition, the aesthetic response is strongly intuitive, a process beyond sensation and emotion that allows the perception of a meaningful whole greater than the sum of its parts. Although intuition is a slippery function that resists explication, it seems to be related to the ability to comprehend through metaphoric images that arise spontaneously in response to less empirical information than analytic thinking would require. Aesthetics is concerned not only with what governs these particular experiences of sense, heart, and image, but with the impulse to reflect these experiences in expressive form. Reason and Hawkins (1988) associated aesthetic forming with connotative thinking in contrast to denotative or scientific thinking. They described connotative thinking as "the elaboration of feeling and emotional imagery and intuition into created form and expression" (1988, p. 82).

In research, if the guiding question points toward data drawn heavily from sensory, emotional, or intuitive processes, artistic inquiry done by a researcher with well-developed aesthetic consciousness may be the best way to assess and express its meaning. This kind of consciousness will be necessary to guide the creation of a form that effectively communicates qualities that could not be better conveyed in other ways.

APPRECIATION OF QUALITIES AND FORM. The awareness developed through heightened sensation, emotion and intuition enables the discriminating appreciation of qualities. Discrimination is a fine-tuning, like the ability to hear the difference between sharp, flat or perfectly pitched notes. The ability to perceive how these qualities are arranged in relation to each other (i.e. notes making a melody) is what allows the appreciation of form.

A form is sometimes created in response to a practical function, as in the form of a functional chair or pitcher. With aesthetic consciousness, we are able to perceive the qualities, form, and value of an object as *independent* of any function except its artistic one (Fraliegh, 1987). (This doesn't mean that it necessarily has no other function or value.) An artistic function inspires the creation of a form that best expresses the desired essential qualities. For instance, an aesthetic attitude does not assume that it is necessary for the form of a thing to correspond to (or look like) any other thing, as it would in representational art. If the work does refer to something else, either literally or symbolically, its aesthetic form must still be able to stand alone. This is a challenge to the practice and acceptance of artistic inquiry, in that the assumptions of the traditional research paradigm are that the methodology follows a predetermined form and that the presentation of findings directly represents discursive answers to logical questions. To embrace artistic inquiry, the aesthetic consciousness of the profession must be revitalized and applied to the production and appreciation of research.

DYNAMIC POLARITIES. Aesthetic consciousness is not a simple, unified kind of awareness that can be easily classified. Instead it is full of dynamic tensions between a range of what seem to be contradictory modes of perception or conceptualization. It is my understanding that flexible movement between the poles of this range, a few examples of which will be given, is one of the things that makes an aesthetic attitude uniquely what it is.

With aesthetic consciousness, we intuitively perceive a phenomenon as inextricably part of a greater whole. For instance, a choreographer knows that the meaning of a dance is determined by more than just its movement. Meaning evolves through the interaction of the different dancers within a context of space, sound, costumes, light, and a broader context of history and culture. However, as Eisner (1995) identified, an aesthetic attitude also allows for "constructive neglect," or attending away from that which the creator/researcher determines is not essential to the perception of the chosen phenomenon. So, rather than removing the phenomenon being studied from its context and controlling the variables impacting it, the artistic researcher may observe how selected aspects of the environment impact the appearance of an object while attending away from other aspects. This is easy to see in the way sunlight changes the appearance of an object over time in a natural setting. An artist sensitive to these changes will not be attending directly to the sound and feel of the wind or the smells in the air, as they are not critical to the perception of light on the object of interest. This dynamic tension between a selective focus and a holistic appreciation of the interactivity of parts is one characteristic of an aesthetic perspective. Related to this is the interactivity between the unique aesthetic values of a particular artist and the aesthetics of the prevailing cultural context. The artist works within a culture, reacts to it, pushes against it, and is subject to its criticism, and yet the form of the work is ultimately determined by his or her independent aesthetic sense.

Another aspect of aesthetic consciousness is the dynamic between separation and empathy in how the artist/researcher understands and conveys the experience of what we could call the research subject. Classic aesthetic perception has been described as one with a sense of distance from the phenomenon, in particular from its potential use to the observer. Distance allows a perspective from which to view the structural characteristics of the observed. From this position, which could be called objectivity, the observer is as free as possible from investment in a particular outcome of the study. At the same time though, the artist/researcher cares passionately about the inquiry. She has a sense of empathy through which she compassionately comprehends the meaning, experience, or feelings of the person or thing under consideration through identifying with it. The empathic emotional resonance between artist/researcher and what is being studied is essential to the convincing artistic communication of its meaning and essential qualities. This is one of the reasons that good dance is able to touch us so deeply. The choreographer has understood something essential about his or her subject through emotional and kinesthetic empathy, but also has been able to move into a position of sufficient separateness to objectively perceive the structural qualities of the emerging dance. Compared to other art forms this is especially challenging, as the dance is literally created in the body of the choreographer. To move beyond this intimacy with the dance, he or she puts it on the body of another or looks in a mirror. If these options are not available or desirable, he or she develops a clear and accurate visual image through an "inner witness" as if looking at the dance from outside her body, thereby achieving the necessary sense of separateness. Yet the dance will always be intrinsically and inseparably part of the choreographer.

Another paradoxical pair of qualities integral to aesthetic consciousness is suspended judgment alternating with evaluation. An open attitude of "anything goes" is necessarily balanced by the assessment of what is good, desirable, or valuable. In observing a phenomenon, the aesthetic perspective provides a certain amount of freedom from judgment in accepting the observed as it is, by simply witnessing the unfolding of the thing without attaching meaning to or evaluating it. If it is too quickly classified by a preexisting set of criteria, the unique qualities of the work may be overlooked. The artist/researcher needs to be able to observe without interpretation, allowing the thing to reveal itself without censure or perceptual restriction and still be able to determine what is "good" or "right" about it according to a particular set of aesthetic criteria. In the qualitative research analysis method of "constant comparison" (Strauss & Corbin, 1990) the researcher shuttles back and forth between open perception and interpretation, allowing them to be impacted by each other. This can be compared to aesthetic consciousness during art-making and the creative process.

Tacit knowing and explicit expression are also engaged in aesthetic consciousness in a complementary manner. We know tacitly those things that we perceive but are not held explicitly and discreetly in consciousness. They are the perceptions that we "attend away from" to perceive other things directly (Polanyi, 1966). We are often unable to verbally express what we know tacitly because it is less-than-consciously embedded in memories of emotion, sensation, and intuition. Artistic expression is therefore one of the best ways to communicate what is known tacitly. Although this kind of communication is not what we would normally think of as explicit, the artist does explicate his or her creative image in the medium being used. The artist/researcher wrestles with the perceptual data, with his or her tacit understanding of it, and with the artistic medium to reveal the essence of the findings as articulately and explicitly as possible.

To work simultaneously from dynamically different styles of consciousness such as these, artistic inquirers must not simply tolerate the tension between them, but must recognize and use their creative potential.

AWARENESS OF AESTHETIC VALUES. In the publication of traditional research, any aesthetic choices are predetermined by scholarly form. Researchers need to know the values of the professional journal in which they are pursuing publication. Likewise the reviewers of submitted research articles are strictly guided by the aesthetic values of the journal.

The aesthetic choices of artists are not regulated in this way, however influenced they may be by the prevailing culture. Therefore, for an artist or critic to exercise aesthetic judgment, they need to know their aesthetic values. Certainly judgments can be made in a haphazard manner, and often are during periods of experimentation or transition. But a work of art with integrity and internal coherence arises from conscious discrimination in making aesthetic choices, whether guided by theory, cultural imperative or individual taste.

In producing artistic inquiry, the aesthetics of the researcher, of the venues for publication or presentation, and of the research consumers must be taken into consideration. At this time, all three of these groups associated with the production and presentation of research in dance/movement therapy are probably less than clear about what their aesthetic values might be in regard to artistic inquiry.

THE AESTHETICS OF DANCE/MOVEMENT THERAPY

"It is not unreasonable to encourage our scholars to apply the aesthetic principles of the profession to scholarship" (McNiff, 1986, p. 283). If dance/movement therapists are to apply their aesthetic principles to scholarship, they must be conscious of what they are. One way to ascertain aesthetic principles is to ask what one values about the collection of experiences that are dance/movement therap, and determine which of these valued experiences can be described as aesthetic. That would require recognition of what is considered beautiful or what qualities and forms are appreciated.

A clinician's aesthetic values could be further assessed by being aware of what is looked for, what is perceived well, what is encouraged in clients. It may require a conceptual shift for some readers to accept that aesthetic values play a part in the methods of the profession, but with aesthetic consciousness alert, they will see these values engaged in assessment, treatment planning, and the most common interventions. This list is not intended to be exhaustive or authoritative, but invites readers to consider these aesthetic values as active in their professional practices. While enumerating these aesthetics, I will also help readers imagine how they might be applied to research by providing examples.

THE IMAGE OF HEALTH. Much of what dance/movement therapy values is associated with a particular image of health, as Ellen Dissanayake (1995) points out is true of human aesthetics in general. She has theorized that qualities such as brilliance of color, luster, quickness, strength, grace, flexibility, and smoothness are all qualities of health and youth and, for evolutionary reasons, are attractive to humans. Dance/movement therapists have an image of health that has similar aesthetic qualities such as coordination, flexibility, and a wide yet balanced range of affect expressed through bodily rhythms and efforts. In research then, if scales are developed to determine progress toward treatment goals, it is very likely that an aesthetic image of health will be playing an active part. The presence of this image of health will be evident in many of the following aesthetic descriptors.

FREEDOM OF FORM. The aesthetic roots of dance/movement therapy are in modern dance, especially the early expressionist pioneers, such as Duncan, Wigman, and Graham, who rejected the classical ballet form and were committed to individual freedom of expression. One of the most beautiful features of dance/movement therapy is how it encourages the creative participation of the client. Dance/movement therapists embrace the unique in each individual and often resist classifying people by standardized norms or diagnoses. Variety rather than conformity is encouraged in group movement experiences. Dance/movement therapists are comfortable in the realm of the imagination and understand how to facilitate its expression in movement.

In research, it follows that what Eisner and Barone (1997) called personal style, or the unique expression of the individual artist/researcher would also be valued. This might mean embracing unique forms of research that communicate a variety of experience rather than looking for standardization of affirmation of norms.

MEANING IN FORM. For dance/movement therapists, as for the pioneers of modern dance, expressive movement is imbued with and inseparable from both personal and universal meaning. They are not moved or impressed by beautiful but empty or vapid dance technique. They appreciate meaningful movement.

Dance movement therapy does not seem to have identified with the "art for art's sake," formalist aesthetic of choreographers like Merce Cunningham, which values only the structural aspects of the art, rather than the meaning of its content. I have also yet to see any evidence of dance/movement therapy embracing a postmodern aesthetic such as that described by art therapist Rosalie Politsky as one of "impur[ity], ambiguity, contradiction, complexity, incoherence and inclusiveness" (1995, p. 312). This is not to say that dance/movement therapy is not capable of moving in that direction, or that dance/movement therapists may not be trained in structuralist or postmodern dance, or that a postmodern aesthetic has no value for the practice of dance/movement therapy. Recall the importance of being able to suspend judgment and interpretation of meaning so as to allow the dance in and of itself to evolve. This is a strength of a postmodern perspective, which resists attaching meaning to movement and can loosen the hold of overbearing interpretation from any particular theoretical perspective.

McNiff's criticism of research that is "unintelligible, fragmented, and loosely associated" (1987, p. 288) confirms that meaningful coherence of form is one of his aesthetic values as an artist/researcher. As Eisner wrote, "What one seeks . . . is the creation of an evocative form whose meaning is embodied in the shape expressed" (1981, p. 6). Like the image of health, this appreciation of form that is inseparable from meaning will also be evident throughout this explication of other aesthetic values of dance/movement therapy.

PATTERNS. Expressive movement that forms recognizable patterns is very close to being dance. This is one reason why dance/movement therapists are particularly sensitive to patterns arising in movement. Repetitions and rhythms help organize chaotic movement and make communication through movement easier. In dance/movement therapy, movement is led in repeatable patterns. Patterns are discerned in the movement of clients to help ascertain its message. In research, the discrimination of patterns is essential to the emergence of meaning in the data.

One form or pattern that seems to have particular value to dance/movement therapy is the circle. It is the form most frequently used in groups of all sorts, both while moving and while talking. Aside from its functional qualities, such as equal visibility and hearing for all members, it has aesthetic strength. It conveys many of the aesthetic values of dance/movement therapy, such as coherence, wholeness, spatial containment, smoothness, strength, flexibility, and the cyclical nature of process and pattern. Human groups tend to congregate naturally in the circle because it is such a strong form. The circle could be incorporated in many aspects of the research process, from gathering coresearchers in the circle to generate data, to arranging data in circles as part of analysis, to presenting findings in a circular format. The aesthetic power of the circle could add strength to the form and presentation of the research.

STORY. In dance, "the narrative is meant to express the essence of a thing, idea, person, or whatever is being reflected upon" (Blumenfeld-Jones, 1995, p.398). Dance/movement therapists often look for the essence of meaning in the embodied stories told by patients. Fragmented, disjointed, contradictory qualities of form (in the body or in the dance) tend to alert therapists to disturbance or disconnection from meaning. Therefore it seems that they value narrative, and the more internally coherent the better. (Note that coherent does not necessarily mean linear, as story in expressive movement or dance is often portrayed non-discursively). Movement or dance invites understanding by effectively embodying the meaning of the mover's story. In research the narrative of dance could shed light on the affective experiences of clients or on researcher practitioners.

AUTHENTICITY. Dance/movement therapists, in looking for meaning in the mover's narrative, are not looking for movement that is necessarily pretty or graceful, but movement that Eisner and Barone (1997) would call *expressive language*. Authenticity, revelation, posture-gesture merger, emotional connection, or what Heidegger described as beauty in the unconcealedness of being is what is being sought. As "connoisseurs" of movement, these qualities are dance/movement therapy's criteria for truth *and* beauty. I don't believe there is a practicing dance/movement therapist who does not know from experience that even the simplest or most awkward authentic movement can be profoundly beautiful. In research then, perhaps the reader can imagine using this kind of truth criterion to assess the validity of the data or to present findings.

DEPTH. Related to seeing beauty in authenticity is the appreciation of qualities that reveal the depth of a form. Dance/movement therapists look into the depths of a person's experience rather than settling for a shallow understanding. They encourage their clients toward deeper insight through the therapeutic process. The unconscious or the depth of a person's psyche is familiar territory to most dance/movement therapists, who treasure what can be uncovered there. The corresponding characteristic in research might be a desire to explore the profound in the phenomenon in question, perhaps through in-depth interviews or authentic movement. Often times numerical findings are like labels put on the surface of a box, leaving us wanting to know more about what's inside. Artistic inquiry can open the box and explore deeply into its contents.

VITALITY. Dance has some unique aesthetic qualities compared to other art forms because it is embodied. It is grounded in what Fraleigh called the "vital movement sensibility" of choreographer, dancer, and audience.

> We realize in dance the esthetic in the kinesthetic. We realize beauty or other desirable qualities through movement sensibility, or the kinesthetic sense—our ability to sense energy, temporality, and spatial locatedness through bodily movement . . . . Dance must involve the kinesthetic at vital and intelligent levels. (Fraleigh, 1987, p. 46)

Dance/movement therapists value vitality, a quality that reflects affirmation of and connection to life. Its presence is assessed kinesthetically. Likewise this "kinesthetic aesthetic" might be used to assess the "vitality validity" of data and findings. To be useful for research, this assessment must be used with what Fraleigh referred to as intelligence, which I understand to be a combination of awareness, skill, articulation, and application.

THE BODY. Dance/movement therapists spend a lot of their professional time looking at bodies, and I believe for the most part the appearance of the human body is something that dance/movement therapists appreciate. Unfortunately, intrinsic to an inheritance from dance may be a particular aesthetic that has dictated an unrealistic, sylph-like image for women's bodies. Although this dictate may be somewhat successfully resisted on an intentional level, the image of the ideal dancer's body may still have some lingering impact on dance/movement therapy's communal aesthetic. In research, if the body is used as a vehicle for presentation because it is enjoyed and valued aesthetically, an awareness must be maintained that the value placed on a particular body image may distort the accurate communication of findings. (Bill T. Jones' choice around this aesthetic dilemma is addressed in Chapter 6.)

Dance/movement therapists also value the body as a vehicle of expression and a rich source of information. Assumptions such as "the body doesn't lie" and concepts like "body ego" and "body memory" are generally accepted. Sensory experience through the body is trusted as essential to knowing oneself. Dance/movement therapists assess meaning through the expression of the body. Therefore they trust the body as a source of data and rely on their understanding of body experience as a form of data analysis.

WHOLENESS. Dance/movement therapy has a holistic approach to the person. The value of wholeness is reflected in aspiration toward a balanced use of movement qualities, integration of the body as a whole, and all parts working in harmony as they would in dance. The theoretical foundation of dance/movement therapy is based on a confidence in the interconnection and integration of body, mind, and spirit. For example, dance/movement therapists are wary of communication that is overintellectualized; they work toward emotional expression that is mediated by cognitive functioning; they may be concerned if they sense a spiritual void in a client's world view.

For research this suggests seeking a holistic view of the person as subject and as researcher. It might mean gathering data from multiple, inseparable realms of the person's experience and not splitting it into discrete variables because they are more easily controlled. Appreciating interconnection and harmony indicates an understanding that the parts cannot be divided from the whole and still provide an accurate reflection of the person or phenomenon.

CONTEXT. In dance, the meaning of every gesture, every posture, and even stillness is part of a larger context that is defined by the rest of the body, the other dancers, the staging, the other dances in the program, the history, culture, location, audience, and so forth. All of these aspects of context are inextricable from the story or the formal aspects of the dance. In dance/movement therapy, we value knowing our clients through attention to a context similarly constructed of family, personal history, culture, environment, witnesses, time, and more. Research that attends to contextually determined meaning will focus on the subject of interest without isolating it from contextual influences.

Some aspects of context are given, and some we create. In dance/movement therapy, there is an awareness that movement is always done here, in this moment, that this moment is like no other, and that the movement done now will never be done again. This makes every movement uniquely precious and deserving of full care and attention. Dance/movement therapists make every effort to honorably contain this ephemeral experience within a predictable time and space frame. Therefore they value and create a space that is comfortable, clean, safe, pleasing to the eye, and free of competing sensory distractions. They may be particularly sensitive to its color, furnishings, spatial arrangement, lighting, sound: all of which are part of an aesthetic consciousness. In terms of time, they perceive and value the supportive patterns created by beginnings, middles, and endings. They are sensitive to transitions and the timing of interventions. Like space, the artful use of time is also part of an aesthetic consciousness that can be applied to research as well.

In the gathering of research data, time and space aesthetics do much to determine the feeling of the research milieu. The use of space and timing in dialogues between people could potentially be observed and analyzed from an aesthetic perspective, the way one would view a dance. If artistic presentation of research findings is attempted, attention to spatial considerations such as audience location, dimensions of the space, visibility, staging, and display arrangement will be important to the communication effectiveness. Features of time such as length of presentation, timing and rhythm of changes in the display, and effective beginnings and endings will also influence the impact of the research on viewers.

MUSIC. Most dance/movement therapists are highly attuned to the profound relationship between movement and music. Choice of music for therapeutic purposes involves a highly complex set of criteria very much based on an aesthetic understanding of how dance and music interrelate. Two of the most frequent uses of music are as a powerful emotional catalyst and an organizer of expressive movement.

Music then could be considered at least as a medium to enhance the communication of research findings. The addition of music to the presentation of visual data is especially effective, as the musical soundtracks of film and video so vividly demonstrate. It is not hard to imagine an exhibition of patient art work or photos of patient movement having musical support to organize and increase the affective impact of the presentation.

SKILL AND DISCIPLINE. McNiff wrote, "the methods of art demand discipline and skill" (1987, p. 288). In dance, the skills of the performer are easy to identify, obviously valued, and are the result of years of disciplined training. The skills of the choreographer are somewhat harder for the observer to identify, take some training to appreciate, yet also take years of experience for the artist to develop. In dance/movement therapy, where the technical dance skills and choreographic production of clients and therapists seem to be minimally appreciated, what skills are valued?

The skills that the practice of dance/movement therapy encourage in our clients are embedded values regarding health and creativity. One value that could be perceived aesthetically is the intentional, articulate expression of feelings through movement and words. Much of the work of a dance/movement therapist is focused on assisting the client in developing an expressive movement vocabulary.

The aesthetic skills that are valued in the therapist include the ability to accurately reflect the movement qualities of the client. This entails the intelligent use of kinesthetic empathy as well as the observational skills necessary to see movement in detail and to reproduce it in the therapist's body. One particular kind of observational skill that is valued is the discipline of mindful witnessing, a skill that requires aesthetic awareness as well as other aspects of consciousness. The ability to verbally describe movement to others who may not have a movement-based vocabulary is also highly valued. This is a skill equivalent to that needed by the art/dance critic, which is, as Eisner pointed out, valuable for a researcher. The skills mentioned combine to potentially be especially valuable if we consider the researcher as the primary research tool. Obviously, movement observation is one of dance/movement therapy's unique and most frequently used methods of gathering data. The re-creation of movement, however, is rarely used as a form of presentation of research findings and is worth serious consideration as it is one of the professions' greatest skills.

THE GENERAL IN THE PARTICULAR. One assumption of art-based inquiry in other fields is that the "general resides in the particular" (Eisner, 1981, p. 7). This claim is true for all the arts in that they portray unique individual instances yet also communicate the universal or essence of being of the person, thing, or phenomenon portrayed. In dance, we see the particular movements of this dancer or that character, but we know that a universal character is being revealed in whom we can see aspects of ourselves or the human condition. Dance/movement therapists learn about the larger human condition through their individual clients and see patterns of movement, behavior, thought, affect, life circumstances, or images that speak of the general in the particular. A case study is the kind of research that could tell a particular client or practitioner's story through dance and would also awaken an understanding of more general truths about the therapeutic process through the art form.

AESTHETIC CHOICES OF THE ARTIST/RESEARCHER

An aesthetic approach to research requires perceiving the research as a work of art in formation. Because the form is not predetermined, artistic inquiry involves the creation of new forms that "help us notice what we have learned not to see" (Eisner, 1995, p. 3).

> What artistic approaches [to research] seek is to exploit the power of form to inform . . . . Form is regarded as a part of the content of what is expressed and bears significantly on the kinds of meanings people are likely to secure from the work. (emphasis added, Eisner, 1981, p. 7)

Aesthetic determination refers to all the choices made throughout the research process that are based on the effectiveness of mediums, forms, and contexts to address the various needs of the inquiry. For example, the researcher will need to choose what medium will best capture the qualities inherent in the data; what medium is most sensitive to the subtle impressions of the patterns emerging from the data gathered; and what medium will best reflect the essence of the meaning derived. Once the mediums are selected, decisions around form will need to be made at every step along the way, but especially in the presentation of findings. The qualities of the context (i.e., professional publication, conference, gallery, classroom, auditorium, electronic communication) in which to present the research must be chosen to best highlight its message and communicate to the desired audience.

CONFLICTING MOTIVATIONS AND CHOICES. Artists often have very personal, emotional, intuitive, or sensual questions that guide their explorations. How these interface with aesthetic motivations is one of the most fascinating aspects of art. It is the task of the artist to find the form that best addresses all of his or her questions, and the effectiveness of the form to do so is the goal of the work. The strength or integrity of the form transforms the personal, emotional, or sensual questions of the artist into aesthetic ones. For instance, an emotionally charged but weakly formed dance becomes a personally cathartic expose´ for the artist and may be meaningless for the audience. A strong form, created through the aesthetic choices of a skilled artist, can contain the affect, transcend the personal, and still be an emotionally powerful piece.

All aesthetic decision-making "exploits the potential of selectivity and emphasis to say what needs saying" (Eisner, 1981, p. 8). Not all data speak equally fluently, and for that reason, may not be included in the analysis. "Poetic truths" (Jones, 1997) are those artistic expressions that capture an essence of meaning and so are most useful according to aesthetic reasoning. This is a very different kind of reasoning than would be used to determine the inclusion or exclusion of scientific data and requires a major shift in understanding to appreciate. In artistic inquiry, clear methodological guidelines are not available that determine how data are selected. The bottom line is only a declaration that the choices are based on the artist/researcher's aesthetic values and the desire to let the data speak authentically.

Thus, an issue that arises when we consider research as a work of art is the interface between aesthetic and ethical motivations. One of the characteristics of both art and science is their tendency to push beyond limits, any limits, including those established by cultural beliefs and social norms. A very critical development in the history of scientific research has been the governmental regulation of experimental methods to prohibit science from doing harm to human subjects while zealously pushing into new areas of knowledge. There have been no parallel regulations in art (other than the laws that protect all citizens from harm), which would result in censorship, although there are those who believe it is necessary. Certainly, if an artist declares himself or herself to be a researcher and has a professional affiliation, as dance/movement therapists do, then any regulations that apply to research with human subjects would apply to methods used in artistic inquiry as well.

But what of more subtle forms of pushing beyond ethical limits? Do poetic truths tell the same kind of truths that we come to expect in daily discourse? (For that matter, do scientific truths?) Does poetic license give the artist the right to creatively manipulate the verbal or nonverbal statements of coresearchers or participants? What protection do informants or clients have against their words, emotions, and actions being misrepresented by the artist/researcher whose primary interest is in aesthetic form?

Obviously the reasons for doing artistic inquiry are not purely aesthetic, and this is one thing that distinguishes it from art. One of the goals of doing artistic inquiry is to create a form that best communicates the information gained through the inquiry. But our ultimate goal is a fuller, deeper, and more accurate understanding about how dance/movement therapy can best meet the needs of those with whom we work. In dance/movement therapy, we have many research questions that may or may not have aesthetic components. If we frame these questions (or some of them) aesthetically, and address them through artistic forms, we need to remain conscious of our ultimate goal to understand how dance/movement therapy helps our clients. Together, the coresearchers, the professional community, and the research consumers need to regulate these motivational conflicts in such a way that does no harm to subjects, researchers, or the public.

This said, it is also essential to the promotion of artistic inquiry to remember that one of the essential differences between artistic inquiry and other research lies in the nature of what art is. We do not expect art to represent literally, but metaphorically. Even the most representational art is still only a version of what seems to be reality. Picasso was once accused by a man of creating nothing but distortions. The man pulled out a photograph of his wife, claiming that it was what his wife *really* looked like, in contrast to the cubist representations that Picasso made of women. Picasso's reply was, "She's awfully small. And flat" (Nachmanovitch, 1990, p. 117-118). The man saw the photograph as an accurate representation of his wife because it showed the features he was accustomed to seeing in a manner that was also familiar to him. Art does not always show what we are used to seeing, and it shows us in ways that expand our perception of the things and events it portrays. This does not mean that what it finds and reveals is any less true.

Some of the difficulties derived from various interpretations of "reality" might be eased if artistic researchers were to inform participants that they were working within an artistic framework. Sharing the methodology with participants would also contribute to their understanding of how their contributions might be used and represented. Participants would then be prepared if the findings of the research were presented artistically. In Chapter 6 it will be illustrated how Bill T. Jones framed his methodology for the participants in his inquiry.

AESTHETIC INFLUENCES IN "IDENTIFYING STUDENT ATTITUDES AND FEELINGS ABOUT DOING RESEARCH"

In the research project described fully in the Appendix there were at least nine aesthetic values that influenced the choices I made in gathering and analyzing data, and in presenting the findings. The first (1) was the choice to repeatedly use the circle as a form to arrange people and data throughout the course of the project. This was in part due to another aesthetic choice: awareness, and respect for the context (2), which was an Antioch graduate-level class that is most often conducted in a circle. Therefore it was a familiar working form for all participants. But the circle also allowed for the display of visual data (squiggle drawings) and the discussion of textual data in a cohesive, non-hierarchical, community-reinforcing manner. An exception to the circle format occurred when I (alone) displayed the statistical data that I (alone) had tabulated on the chalkboard. The format then reverted to that used in a traditional educational setting with the teacher standing at the head of a class of seated, receptive, rather than active, learners. Clearly these choices of form reflect the meaning of the interactions within the context.

The data and its meaning emerged within the natural context of the classroom in which the research course would be taught, with all the regular class members and no outside researchers present. Limits around time and space (3) were then determined in part by the natural context. Choices were also made as to the length of each section of the inquiry based on the time necessary to draw a picture and to really look at a group of pictures long enough to see qualitative similarities. Likewise, the time needed to analyze the data was determined by the discussion's natural flow, stimulated by sharing the visual and textual data. I have already discussed the choices made around space, that is, the circle.

The choice to gather and analyze three different kinds of data and present them in three different ways reflected a value of wholeness (4) that was at least partially aesthetic. I valued the information I would gain from the students' self-expression in image, words, and numbers and hoped to integrate their emotional, intuitive, and cognitive responses toward an understanding of their educational needs.

In asking them to draw and write in free style I communicated an appreciation for the unique and imaginative (5), rather than the standardized. In directing them to look for patterns (6) in the small clusters of art works that they formed, I again conveyed an appreciation for uniqueness and imagination, as well as an aesthetic assumption that meaning could be found in form (7). My choice to have them share their written responses to research, which resulted in story telling about their research experiences, reflected the aesthetic value of narrative (8). And finally, confident that each particular artwork and each story would convey some truth about the whole class' feelings through shared themes and created dances, I expressed my belief that the general can be found in the particular (9).

I also made informed aesthetic choices in determining the mediums and the methods used to elicit responses used as data. I knew that wide-tipped colored marking pens would be easy to use and would facilitate the quick and bold response to the particular question I asked. The directions I gave (to create a non-representational drawing that came from a bodily response rather than a cognitive one) were based on artistic experience and awareness that the squiggle drawing would best express an emotional response. Its simplicity and directness would lend itself well to analysis by non-artists in a quick, rewarding manner that did not rely on aesthetic expertise.

The component of the project that involved the production of drawings was clearly aesthetically motivated by me, the primary researcher. I have long known that this method is effective in eliciting response, and I have a certain insatiable aesthetic curiosity and pleasure in witnessing these unique little creations take form. This overarching delight in the creative process was an aspect of the research question that remained unexplicated, although it was influential in the choice of methods. It is a core characteristic of who I am as a clinician and as a researcher, and thus the method chosen authentically represented me, my values, my skills, and my work.

AESTHETIC INFLUENCES IN "RESEARCHER AS ARTIST/ARTIST AS RESEARCHER"

One of the challenges faced by artistic inquirers is finding an appropriate forum that is flexible enough to incorporate nontraditional forms of presentation. Professional journals have been one of the most common means of distributing research findings, but are traditionally not very flexible in regard to innovative and imaginative forms. As part of a broadening attitude toward research forms, in 1995, "Researcher as artist/artist as researcher" (Finley & Knowles) was published in the first volume of *Qualitative Inquiry*, an interdisciplinary journal seeking "cutting edge manuscripts on qualitative research that transcend disciplinary, racial, ethnic, gender, national, and paradigmatic boundaries, *including manuscripts that experiment with nontraditional forms, contents, and modes of representation*" (emphasis added, Denzin & Lincoln, 1995, p. 3).

Authors Susan Finley and Gary Knowles contributed a collaborative article in which they explored how they, as researchers, "were each guided by [their] past, very strong aesthetic and artistic experiences" (p. 110). In a conversational style that included the "voices" of others who had written on the topic as well, they described how their backgrounds in the arts "shaped [their] thinking" (p. 110) about research. In their words, "the result is a postmodern, postcolonial manuscript that generates meaning not only through its content but also through the form in which the content is displayed" (1995, p. 111).

The form they used is completely textual, but uses space in a nontraditional manner, by arranging the contributions of different interlocutors in different locations on the page. Finley's narrative runs along the left column, Knowles' along the right, their collaborative writing holds the traditional full-page location, and other contributors' voices, in the form of quotations, are indented from each margin. In this manner the authors tried to convey how "voices mingle in polyphonic conversation" (1995, p. 111). Finley's and Knowles' first-person narratives are less formal and more personal than a traditional research article would permit, and this, in combination with the spatial arrangement, demonstrates innovation guided by aesthetic sensibilities that can be presented within the format of a professional journal.

I found the acknowledgment of their aesthetic motivations and choices especially valuable as a model for future descriptions of methodology, though it was not as extensive as I would have liked to see. The statement that "the arrangement of the text on the page accentuates the possibility that the reader may find multiple points of entry into the text" communicated the desire to challenge a strictly discursive aesthetic. The arrangement, however, did not sufficiently motivate me to depart from a linear reading of the article.

Similarly, the authors declared that these innovations represented a rejection of the "'logic' of traditional sociological writing" and referred to the ephemeral form of conversation that is "often irrational in its composition" (1995, p. 111). They went on to disclose that they also envisioned the text "performed on a stage crowded with performers . . . eschewing linearity, forgoing the temporal and causal restraints engendered by acts and scenes" and instead engaging in "free-wheeling conversation" (p. 111).

Did the aesthetic intention and the choices made by the researchers serve their research purpose? Despite how active their imaginations may have been in the aesthetic choices made, I found the resulting manuscript richer in content than it was innovative and provocative in form. The form did not interfere with the content, but I'm not sure it contributed intrinsically to it. What I felt the form, and even more so the declared rationale for it, did was to locate the authors in a movement challenging traditional forms of research. If this was their purpose, it was served.

SUMMARY

In this chapter, aesthetics was defined as the discriminating appreciation of qualities reflected in form. In attempting to shed light on aesthetic consciousness, four of its characteristics were described: a heightened awareness borne of experience with sensation, emotion and intuition; a strong appreciation of form; the ability to work fluidly within or between dynamic polarities of consciousness; and an awareness of one's aesthetic values.

Fourteen examples of aesthetic values of dance/movement therapists were suggested:

1. The image of health

2. Freedom of form

3. Meaning in form

4. Patterns

5. Story

6. Authenticity

7. Depth

8. Vitality

9. The body

10. Wholeness

11. Context

12. Music

13. Skill and discipline

14. The general in the particular

In Chapter 7, the discussion about the application of aesthetics to the evaluation of artistic inquiry will suggest that it is most appropriate to use the aesthetic criteria of dance/movement therapists to evaluate AI done in the field. This would necessitate the acknowledgment of some generally agreed on aesthetic values of the profession, like those outlined above. In producing artistic inquiry, consideration would also need to be given to the aesthetics of the venues within which its presentation is pursued, such as conferences, theaters, or galleries.

The present chapter concludes with a discussion of two research projects that illustrate the aesthetic feature of artistic inquiry: the first was my exploration into the attitudes of DMT students toward research and the second an article by Finley and Knowles about the internal dialogue between researcher and artist selves and how it influences the research.

In my desire to promote ethical as well as aesthetic motivations, I suggested that most critical is whether the inquiry addresses our ultimate goal of greater understanding about dance/movement therapy and its support to those in need. These questions will be revisited in the final chapter on the evaluation of artistic inquiry.

The next chapter integrates the defining characteristics of artistic inquiry discussed up to this point to describe a work by Bill T. Jones that I believe meets all three criteria, which once again are:

1. Inquiry that is aesthetically motivated and determined.

2. Inquiry that uses and acknowledges a creative process.

3. Inquiry that uses artistic methods of data collection, analysis, and presentation.

The view of Jones' work presented herein is clearly mine, based on the principles I have outlined thus far in this explication of artistic inquiry. *Still/Here*, like any work of art, has a unique meaning of its own that cannot be contained by the purposes and conceptualizations of any one person. I hope that my interpretation of his work in no way limits its ability to communicate its larger truth to any who may read or be influenced by my understanding of it.

Chapter 6

ARTISTIC INQUIRY: BILL T. JONES'
STILL/HERE

The profoundest questions that I can ask can be answered with other people, who are not in the dance world...For me, as a person who has to deal with his own possible early death, I was looking for people who were dealing with the same thing. I said, "Let's go out and deal with the people who know, who are front line."

What do you know? What do you know that I don't know? What do we have in common that the average person does not? Tell me it. Show me it. And I'm going to take it, going to make it songs, make it movement.

(BILL T. JONES IN MOYERS, 1997)

INTRODUCTION

IN THIS STATEMENT, Jones declared his driving questions and the purposes of his inquiry. When *Still/Here* (the multimedia work resulting from this inquiry) was first performed in 1994, no such disclosure was part of the theatrical presentation, and so audiences and critics were left to conjecture as to his motivations. This work, about living with terminal illness, incited a debate in the dance world that some compared in significance to the controversy about censorship created by Mapplethorpe's photography (Duffy, 1995; Temin, 1997). The disturbance was touched off not simply by the piece itself, but by an acerbic article in the *New Yorker* by the outspoken dance critic Arlene Croce, who refused to see the work because it was, she declared, "victim art" (Croce, 1994). A flurry of response and counter-response followed, centering primarily around whether the piece was or was not "victim art" (Duffy, 1995; Hering, 1995; Siegel, 1996; Sims, 1996; Shapiro, 1995; Teachout, 1995; Yablonsky, 1995).

In 1997, Bill Moyers created a documentary for television that built upon video footage of Jones working with people who had life-threatening illnesses in his Survival Workshops that were held in preparation for *Still/Here*. Moyers included intimate interviews with Jones about his motivations and methods for creating *Still/Here*. He also recorded emotionally rich dance improvisations by Jones in response to Moyers' request that he "do" what he asked his Survival Workshop participants to do in describing their lives through dance. This documentary did not address the issue of victim art, but offered an alternative view of Jones' work on *Still/Here* that seems to have marked an end of the murmuring in the art world about the uses and misuses Jones may have made of people who were living with terminal illnesses. The interview instead portrayed Jones as a compassionate artist, motivated by a drive toward deep, if not spiritual understanding, that had not been recognized or identified in earlier discussions.

I include this description of how *Still/Here* stirred the media dialogue to provide some sense of what is called the creative *press* of the time, and an indication of how the work pushed the edges of what was considered acceptable "art." My objective is not to determine if Jones' work was victim art or not, though the reviews and essays do provoke aesthetic and ethical issues that I will address in the concluding chapter. My intention here is only to suggest that the combined process and product of *Still/Here* is an instance of artistic inquiry that satisfies all three defining criteria of the genre, each of which will be addressed individually. I draw my understanding of Bill T. Jones as an artistic inquirer and his dance/theater piece *Still/Here* as artistic inquiry from four primary resources: (1) a full-length, videotaped representation of *Still/Here* by Gretchen Bender and Bill T. Jones (1996); (2) a documentary, *Bill T. Jones: Still/Here* with Bill Moyers (Moyers, 1997); (3) Jones' keynote address, "A Moving Dialogue," at the 1997

American Dance Therapy Association's Annual Conference; and (4) Jones' 1995 book, *Last Night on Earth*.

I will be referring extensively to Jones' own description of his work from these four sources to support my identification of *Still/Here* as artistic inquiry. As far as I know, this is not a label that he has given his work, and though he did describe the Survival Workshops as "about research" he has also clearly stated that "from the beginning it was about the art" (Jones, 1997).

JONES' USE OF ARTISTIC METHODS OF INQUIRY

Artistic methods of data collection. In his book, Jones outlined what can be understood as the sample demographics and research methodology of this project:

> We conducted 14 workshops in 11 cities. Two of them for children: one in New York and one right here in Philadelphia. The participants were of all ages, classes, races, sexual preferences and states of health. The youngest participant was eleven, the oldest was 74. All were facing or had faced life-challenging situations.
>
> I began each workshop by introducing myself and stating my diagnosis, and reiterating what they might already have known as to why I was there and what I wanted from them:
>
> "I am not a therapist nor am I a practitioner of any kind. I am here because I feel you have information that I as a man might benefit from and as an artist will be inspired by. Yes, I need my hand held dealing with this thing, as I take my place in the world"
>
> I would then introduce my collaborator Gretchen Bender, and her camera crew, and my companion Bjorn who acted as my assistant. The only other people in the room were usually caregivers or a health care professional in case there was a problem. (Jones, 1995, p. 252-253)

In brief, the workshops then proceeded as follows:

- Introductions
- Warm-ups

- Trust exercises

- Jones performed solo "Twenty-One" with explanation.

- Participants created a choreography of the self with their own verbal captions, answering the request: "Tell me about your life right now in one simple gesture" (Moyers, 1997).

- Draw your lifeline: Participants drew and then walked road maps of their lives, alone and with the group, with landmarks at the time of diagnosis, the present, and the time of death.

- Video portraits were created of each participant telling of their loves and fears.

- Closing circle with discussion and questions, some of which were from Jones to the participants, such as "What have you learned" (Jones, 1997).

As this outline of the workshop indicates, almost all of the movements that Jones gathered were already artistic, poetic, or dance creations made by participants, who in effect became cocreators and coresearchers. He may not have acknowledged them as such literally, but seemed to treat the participants as experts about their experiences, drawing out their stories with respect for their authority.

After moving with and videotaping nearly 100 participants of the *Survival Workshops: Moving and Talking about Life and Death* over a period of one year (Moyers, 1997), Jones had generated an extensive collection of powerfully emotional gestures, postures, spatial arrangements, images, words, and stories. It is not hard to see this as a collection of data, or "raw material for dance and song that would be used in a dance theater work to be called *Still/Here*" (Jones, 1997). Jones described the heuristic and artistic nature of his methods: "The movement for *Still/Here* would spring directly from a very specific experience and set of concerns that Gretchen and I documented in the Survival Workshops" (Jones, 1995, p. 252).

ARTISTIC DATA ANALYSIS. Analysis began as participants shared feelings and stories of their lives through movement and words. Jones often mirrored these verbal and nonverbal statements while they were performed. In the video footage of the workshops we can see Jones trying out the movements on his body, reflecting their qualities, and subtly beginning to make the movements his own. At one point he said "I like that. A choreographer looks for that" (Moyers, 1997), reinforcing his identity as an artist and as a collector of data. He repeats a young woman's movement and self-descriptive phrase, clarifying both by asking, "Do you accept that?" She nods, saying simply "Yes" (Moyers). Through this moving dialogue, he has, in effect, confirmed his initial understanding and interpretation of her dance, the way an ethnographer might bring his descriptions and analyses back to the research subjects for verification. This process strengthened what in research would be called the internal validity or the authenticity of the findings.

Like a qualitative researcher who analyzes the data as it is collected rather than waiting until the project is completed, Jones "began choreographing long before there was a large reservoir of material to draw from" (Jones, 1995, p. 256) If we think of the choreography as the method of making meaning out of experience, then the art-making delivered Jones more deeply into understanding. Of this process he said, "Relying on the first workshop...I developed sequences for various combinations of dancers *as I sought a way into the universe of the work"* (emphasis added, Jones, p. 256).

Jones worked with several collaborators, among them media artist/videographer Gretchen Bender, composer Kenneth Frazelle, and rock musician Vernon Reid, each of whom had a part in transforming the data into artistic form. "Through long and searching conversations, Gretchen, Ken and I extracted from the overwhelming mass of material we'd collected the concepts and moods that would define the work" (Jones, 1995, p. 256).

Each collaborator had his or her own unique approach to the transformation, depending on her or his medium and personal artistic style. Jones described Gretchen's discrimination of what data most authentically reflected the stories of the participants:

> Gretchen decided that all material not directly related to the workshop process had to be scrutinized—that only the most essential iconographic imagery should remain in the work. In *Still,* she carefully chose video testimonies, artfully constructed abstractions built on actual workshop episodes, and portraits of each Survival Workshop participant. (1995, p. 258)

Each artist used her or his most highly developed perceptual skills in a connoisseurship or personal style (Eisner, 1991; Barone & Eisner, 1997) that made her or his contribution as a human instrument uniquely valuable and irreplaceable. (This reflects the aesthetic value identified in

Chapter 5 as "freedom of form.") Compare the approaches of Jones' musical collaborators to the use of mechanical or standardized tools in scientific research that intentionally make the contributions of individual researchers interchangeable:

> Whereas Ken had spent much of the fall and winter of 1993-94 viewing the videos of the workshops, Vernon–sensitive even to accidental sounds, such as the rasp and rattle of the participants moving about the workshop space holding the drawings, the "maps" of their lives–was only interested in the audio recording. Using up-to-the-minute electronic techniques, he created moody, pop, jazz, blues riffs as a raster through which actual fragments of survivor's testimonies were heard. (Jones, 1995, p. 256)

> Vernon will cut and paste, repeat and reconfigure sounds and voices, suggesting a world that cruises inexorably forward and ultimately soars. (p. 262)

Note the similarity between Vernon's methods and the cutting and pasting of a qualitative researcher analyzing narrative data. Both seek to uncover and then construct meaning in a way that captures the essence of the story, though Vernon's methods are explicitly artistic.

ARTISTIC PRESENTATION OF FINDINGS. Much like other researchers, Jones began the performance of *Still/Here* by defining his terms, allowing his audience to follow along in an informed manner:

> In the prelude to *Still*, the company performs a straightforward exhibition of several survivor's gesture sequences, naming each gesture's author and reciting its verbal caption. This is a blatant reference to the Survival Workshop and serves as a glossary of sorts in viewing the work that follows. (Jones, 1995, p. 259)

But unlike most researchers, one of Jones' defining purposes was to communicate feelings. A work of art does not, however, simply express a feeling in a formless catharsis of emotional material. Art gives intentional shape to affect, one of the essential qualities of an experience. Jones reflected on the relationship between feeling and form in this description of his formative process in *Still/Here*:

> The thought behind the movement, that is, the form of the piece, was just as important as the feeling engendered by the piece...Our different thoughts in a situation can result in drastically different feelings, and so I place (in this piece) a great deal of importance on the thought process as represented by

the choreography, trusting that feelings come out of form. (Jones, 1997)

Art is also not literal, not representational fact-telling like the journalistic reporting and videography of the Moyers documentary, in which the workshop participants and Jones represented themselves and told their own stories. Compare this documentary approach to *Still/Here*, in which

> The dancers . . . would not impersonate the sick and dying, but the many variations of the struggle I learned about through Arnie's illness and death and the illnesses and deaths of numerous others, through my own experience, and through the experiences of the workshop participants. (1995, p. 252)

Jones' statement alludes to one of the essential features of art: the metaphorical representation and synthesis of *qualities*. In *Still/Here* there are two sections, *Still* and *Here*, each with a different feeling quality and a different symbolic purpose. Jones described the artistic choices made to create the qualitative differences between the two sections through the symbolic use of color, costume, words, sound, lighting, setting, gesture, movement style, space, time, and energy. "If *Still* is the interior world of one person or a group of individuals struggling with a troubling revelation, then *Here* parallels the sensation of leaving one's doctor's office with the life-altering news, compelled to ride the New York City subway" (Jones, 1995, p. 261).

> Everything about *Still*–Liz Prince's softly flowing costumes in shades of ivory, pale blue, and beige, lighting designer Robert Wierzel's use of video blue, the pageantlike parade of events, and the music's restrained emotion –is designed to evoke an internal world, a world apart. (Jones, 1995, p. 261)

Contrast this to the qualities evoked in *Here*:

> Prince designed garments that drape less, promise more through provocative seams, seductive fabrics in shades of red, rust, and orange that at once suggest night life, vivacity, and the color of blood. . . . The world of *Here* seems more spacious–a frontier perhaps. . . . Wierzel had a free hand in dramatically changing mood through coloring the cyclorama orange or acid yellow. At one point he transforms the stage with pulsing areas of light that suggest a disco. (Jones, 1995, p. 261)

In describing the work of another of his collaborators, Jones made it explicitly clear how artistic methods uniquely convey the meanings of the stories he witnessed: "In [Ken's] songs, he evoked survivor's revelations, states of mind, moments of intensity, with a power and specificity *only poetry can deliver*" (emphasis added, 1995, p. 256).

Jones did not attempt to reproduce participants' movements or words exactly. Most of what they shared with Jones was artistically manipulated or analyzed and presented in a synthesized state. He described one exception to this: "After an evening of disembodied voices and artfully chosen glimpses of real people, Gretchen and I felt committed to show them, give them faces in a special ritual" in which "the viewer is offered huge, luminous faces in black and white" (p. 265). Even this ritual did not literally show the audience the real people whose experiences were the essence of this art work. Instead it enlarged them, bringing their affective realities intimately close to the viewers.

Are the poetic truths that Jones offered in artistic form really larger than life? Do they effectively point toward something greater than more literal representations could? Or are they simply crafted distortions, seductions, distillations, suggestions, with only a hint of the power that the original participants experienced and shared? This is the challenge the artistic researcher faces, to create what only good art can deliver—*more* than what we can express in linear discourse. Again, as Dewey said, art delivers *more* than we perceive in the original "scattered and weakened" experience. Unlike more traditional forms of research, simply following the prescribed methodological guidelines and using the recommended formulas is not art. The artist finds a new way.

CREATIVE PROCESS

The unusual wealth of information about Jones' creation of *Still/Here* offers a unique opportunity to understand his creative process as an inquirer. This opportunity also makes clear the creative nature of this particular work's methodology, which is at least as well documented as that of a traditional research project.

It is also clear that Jones has repeatedly demonstrated all the characteristics of a creative scientist that were identified by Beveridge (in

McNiff, 1986, see Chapter 4). In terms of what I called the perception phase of the creative process (see Chapter 4), Jones also engaged perceptual openness to and a relational dialogue with the data. His development of innovative methods of inquiry was also obvious.

Most prominent in Jones' descriptions of his work, however, were three characteristics that will be described further in the following sections. They are: (1) faith in the dance as a creative process, (2) self as medium/artist/researcher, and (3) appreciation for and ability to synthesize ambiguity.

FAITH IN THE DANCE AS A CREATIVE PROCESS. From all recent sources it is clear that Jones is a man of faith, perhaps not in any organized religion, but in the "Big Dance" that is life (Jones, 1998) and in the gift of human creativity that brings about the small dances that are reflections of God's greater dance.

Choreographing a dance demands active participation in a process that is bigger than the individual. Most artists would agree that they do not create through self-will or ego-strength alone. When asked by Moyers to extemporaneously make a dance telling of his own moment of death, Jones replied, "Oh, I'm too small" (Moyers, 1997). But he dances anyway, suggesting an awareness that creating is an act of faith that humbles him as an artist, yet holds him and carries him and the dance forward.

Creating a dance that not only conveyed his own experience, but the profound experiences of over a hundred people certainly must have been humbling. Faced with this challenge, Jones relied on the belief an artist must have in his creative process, directing himself to "just make a beautiful dance, an interesting, vital, challenging dance and it will say everything that I learned from Survivors" (Moyers, 1997).

Before he made *Still/Here*, when faced with the despair resulting from the death of his partner Arnie Zane, and with the possible financial ruin of their dance company, Jones was supported by his faith in the creative process and in his company members: "This [the company] was the child that Arnie and I had had, and I would try – at least once more – to supply the necessary information, ask hard questions, and trust that something vital would come into the world" (Jones, 1995, p. 252).

SELF AS MEDIUM/RESEARCHER/ARTIST. The dancer's medium is the body, his or her own, and those of others. When researching/creating through the body, subtleties of sensation, gesture, and posture become sources of meaning (Stinson, 1995). Although the choreographer's mediums also include presentational settings, lights, music, and costumes, he or she is most highly attuned to the stories told by the body. The best choreographers become masters of this embodied narrative by communicating the essence of the stories through their own bodies to their dancers who must in turn make the meaning their own.

Dance and choreography are then like the heuristic processes that Moustakas (1990) described as a form of research. There is no way to separate the experience of the dancer and choreographer from the dance. In terms of research, this could be recognized as the qualitative researchers' method of using themselves as the primary research tool (Eisner, 1991; Maykut & Morehouse, 1994). As an artistic inquirer Jones alluded to this: "My own process involved the intuitive combining of the survivor's gestures to make phrases, plumbing my own body's imagination, or borrowing from existing forms . . . to create expressive dance sequences" (1995, p. 258). Here Jones also referred to using his imagination and intuition, other subjective methods of discovery taken for granted as parts of creative process, but which can also be vital parts of research (Nisbet,1976).

Creating art often involves the transformation of the feelings of the artist into form. In the Moyer's interview, Jones described his experience of communicating his feelings and the internal changes that occurred. It is notably reminiscent of the qualitative researcher who is inevitably altered by the dialogue with the data, the medium, and the audience (Harman, 1996; Lawrence-Lightfoot & Davis, 1997):

> When you craft certain events in time and space they begin to suggest what you feel. Suddenly you are working out what you feel, coping with it. And the feelings change, and you make more. And you're now engaging the world through your work. You're a full citizen again. You're producing. You're talking to people. You're not shut down any more. Your fears are suddenly more manageable because you've abstracted them, maybe. Maybe its a trick, well I say its a survival technique. My work is that dialogue. (Jones in Moyers, 1997)

APPRECIATION FOR AND ABILITY TO SYNTHESIZE AMBIGUITY. Sometimes the feelings experienced by the dancer/artist seem to be paradoxical or contradictory, and the creative task is then one of synthesis, as Jones described in this passage: "At the conclusion of each workshop, I had felt a combination of sober introspection and exhilaration. . . . The choreography for *Still* tried to meld these sensations" (emphasis added, 1995, p. 258).

Synthesis involves not just feelings but also seemingly opposed images, sensations, and concepts. In presenting *Still/Here*, Jones worked with movement and sound in a way that challenged the synthetic process of the observers as well as the artists. Jones' description (1995) of a new "strategy" that he used in some of the multimedia portions of the work illustrated these processes: "I set up a field of movement material and juxtapose it to a text, thereby challenging the viewers to process what they are seeing and hearing simultaneously (p. 262). . . . I grew more confident that the viewer could simultaneously absorb the continued evolution of the dance, the video portraits, and the score's constantly changing voice" (p. 265).

JONES' AESTHETIC MOTIVATION AND JUDGMENT

AESTHETIC CONSCIOUSNESS. It seems obvious that a successful choreographer such as Jones must have a highly developed aesthetic consciousness of the sort described in Chapter 5. Rarely, however, is the public privy to any evidence of this other than what can be inferred from the quality of his or her art works. But because of the unusually articulate autobiographical documentation of Jones' work in writing and video, we do have the opportunity to glimpse what is usually not accessible. The aspect of aesthetic consciousness most salient in these resources is his ability to move between dynamically opposed perceptual and conceptual modes in rapid alternation or to work in them simultaneously.

Particularly valuable to the creation of *Still/Here* was Jones' ability to maintain both a separate and an empathic posture toward the sources of his data. In contrast to the objective posture from which a traditional researcher might strive to observe subjects, Jones witnessed from a state of heightened aesthetic consciousness that literally embodied *both* objective distance *and* kinesthetic empathy. Working in this position is a skill familiar to, if not necessary for, dancers, choreographers, and dance/movement therapists. He described it as:

A time out of time. It is here that all events really reside. This time out of time is available to me only if I locate the place of respite, that vantage point that allows me to witness the swirl of places, events, thoughts, memories, feelings we call the world. By witness I mean to experience, make note of with profound detachment. Some call it a still point, but *this* point's relationship to the swirl is *dance*. It flutters, it pops, it jumps, it flies, it oscillates, it moves. (punctuation reflects Jones' verbal emphasis, Jones, 1997)

Similarly, in his interview with Bill Moyers, Jones described "Here" (as in *Still/Here*) as "the place that I can stand and not be distracted by pain, not be in the future, in the past. I can be loving. I can be responsive" (1997). In the video footage of the Survival Workshops, this place appears much like the actively involved interpersonal attitude of both a dance/movement therapist and a qualitative researcher. We see Jones at his best with the participants when he is genuinely asking them for their stories, listening with rapt attention and subject to no distractions. "I want to see what people come up with from their own humble resources" (Moyers).

Evidence of other dynamic polarities brought together in the creation of *Still/Here* are implicit in the following discussion of aesthetic motivations and choices.

AESTHETIC MOTIVATION. Many things, among them strong emotion, religious experience, social action, and the search for meaning motivate art. But the one motivation that marks art as distinct from other human endeavors is the aesthetic. Jones described one of his aesthetic motivations for the workshops as "vocabulary building." Like many twentieth century dancers, building a unique artistic language is of primary importance. Although he acknowledged that he could gather gestures from any person on the street, Jones preferred the gestures of those with whom he could relate: gestures that would have more meaning for him because of his personal investment in them (Jones, 1997). As is clear in the opening statement of this chapter, this personal investment became the research question for Jones' artistic inquiry.

At times, multiple motivations can work harmoniously together to create effective ends. At other times, motivators such as those mentioned in the previous paragraph can conflict with the aesthetic sensibilities of the artist. In the case of *Still/Here*, two motivations are clearly present: aesthetic and personal need. In evaluating the effectiveness of this dance piece as artistic inquiry, it is important to question if Jones' personal motivations interfered with his aesthetics in any way.

There are those (Croce, 1994; Torossian, 1997) who claim they did.

After the death of his partner Arnie Zane and the discovery of his own HIV status, Jones described himself as in need of "a community that would affirm my place in the world as well as provid[e] me with inspiration" (Jones, 1937). He identified his company's need for a major new work *and* his own need not to be alienated by being HIV positive as the original motivations for *Still/Here*. These purposes were joined to find meaning in the lives of others that resonated with his own experiences through the dance.

From these origins he went on to produce the Survival Workshops. Recall how he clarified his purpose to the participants: "I am here because I feel you have information that I as a man might benefit from and as an artist will be inspired by. Yes, I need my hand held dealing with this thing as I take my place in the world" (Jones, 1997). Again, in these comments he explicates his aesthetic motivation while openly identifying the nature of his personal needs. This declaration is reminiscent of a researcher whose clarity about motivations and investments is as integral to the research project as his or her methodology.

AESTHETIC JUDGMENT. The form that artistic inquiry takes is determined by many aesthetic choices that the artist/researcher makes along the way. Jones has related some of the decisions determining the form of *Still/Here*. One was choosing not to use a specially created company of HIV- positive dancers, but opting "instead for a youthful, healthy, group of dancers," acknowledging that he "ran the risk of denying the truth about debilitating illness." He explained how he resolved this conflict through the aesthetic choice to represent poetic truth through metaphor: "I have now decided that their vitality and physical prowess are an apt and necessary metaphor for the spirit displayed by most survivors I was fortunate to encounter. So [dancer] Torin's bounding resilient undulation *is* [workshop participant] B. Michael speaking" (emphasis added, Jones, 1995, p. 263).

In viewing segments of the Survival Workshops in Moyers' documentary, evidence of the interface between Jones' interpersonal compassion and aesthetic judgment also begins to arise. In his use of trust-building and warm-up exercises, his purpose was "to open a tap that would flow with poetic facts that could be crafted into art" (Jones, 1997). Once this tap was open, the affective verbal and nonverbal statements made by many of the survivors were powerfully compelling. How did Jones then aesthetically select one person's poetic fact from another's, without having to judge the worth or value of one person's *experience* over another's? In art, in traditional research, and in artistic inquiry, the answer to this question lies in the strength and integrity of the methodology and the form. In the same way that the choreographic form holds the intensity of Jones' exploration of his own ultimate death, the declared methodological form needs to safely hold the emotional potential in the researchers' questions and the participants' responses. In research, the chosen method of data analysis transforms the raw data into coherent themes. In Jones' work, the choreography transforms the raw emotion into dance movement and metaphor.

Does Jones achieve a productive balance between his and others' emotional needs and his aesthetic judgment? Is Jones' artistic form strong enough to hold his (and others') very emotional involvement in this question? These questions are about aesthetic evaluation, the job traditionally performed by the art or dance critic. Again, there are those who say yes (Daly, 1997; Gates, 1994; Shapiro, 1995; Siegel, 1996; Yablonsky, 1995), and those who say no (Croce, 1994; Hering, 1995; Teachout, 1995). If this work were artistic inquiry within the profession of dance/movement therapy, answers would need to be provided not by dance critics but by fellow professionals. In addition, whether his findings were effectively communicated to his intended audience would need to be evaluated.

ETHICAL CONCERNS. At one point in his documentary, Bill Moyers (1997) asked Jones how he managed to get complete strangers to open up the way he did. Jones responded by saying "They read my body language. They look me up and down. They say 'Is this guy trying to exploit me?' and I say 'What I want is *everything*'" (emphasis reflects Jones' vocalization). With what appeared on the video documentation to be sincerity, open curiosity, absence of a judgmental attitude, and a passionate desire to hear and accept everything that they had to offer, Jones seemed to create a milieu in which many participants were willing to give "everything" that they could. Is it ethical to engage people in emotional work of this kind that might in some way be harmful if the artist or researcher is not a therapist and is not prepared to deal with the consequences during the process? In the case of the Survival Workshops, Jones seemed to rely on informed consent, his declared purpose and clarity of role. Recall "I am not a therapist or practitioner of any kind" (Jones, 1995, p.253). His years of experience with the methods used and the presence of health-care givers at the workshops seemed to contribute to his sense of security about doing work of an emotionally provocative nature. This may or may not be considered sufficient protection for participants.

Still/Here also stimulates concerns about the interface of profession-al ethics and aesthetic motivations that echo those unpopular ones provoked by critic Arlene Croce. In artistic inquiry, aesthetic judg-ment must be committed to the research question, the form of the evolving artwork, *and* the well-being of the participants. If artistic inquiry is to be accepted by dance/movement therapists it must be clear what the ethical implications are and how it can be used without ethical violation. This and other concerns about the aesthetic, ethical, and methodological evaluation of artistic inquiry, and *Still/Here* in par-ticular, will be explored further in the following chapter.

SUMMARY

The three defining characteristics of artistic inquiry were applied in this chapter to Bill T. Jones' work *Still/Here*. It was illustrated how artistic methods of data collection, data analysis, and presentation of findings could be seen in the Survivor's Workshops and the collabora-tive creation of the piece's choreography, music, costumes, and light-ing. Evidence of Jones' creative research process was drawn from sup-porting texts, lectures, and Bill Moyers' documentary. Finally, it was demonstrated how Jones' aesthetic motivations and judgments deter-mined the form of the inquiry.

Framing *Still/Here* as artistic inquiry evokes many questions, not the least of which is whether it is reasonable to suggest that this kind of research be produced by dance/movement therapists. The next and final chapter of this discussion will examine what it would take for pro-jects similar to this to become part of our research repertoire.

Chapter 7

RECOMMENDATIONS AND CONCLUSION

INTRODUCTION

WITHIN A THERAPEUTIC CONTEXT, dance/movement therapists work creatively, artistically, and aesthetically. The pioneers of dance/movement therapy and many therapists since then have moved dance out of the realm of the purely aesthetic by recognizing its healing qualities. To me, this simultaneous focus on dance *and* helping others is the essence of dance/movement therapy, and in my vision, artistic inquiry is a form of research that can authentically and effectively express this essence.

The final concern of this work is the practical manifestation of this vision, which can be supported through the consideration of three questions:

- When is it appropriate to use artistic methods of inquiry?

- How can artistic inquiry be evaluated?

- If it is a valuable and effective methodology, what more can be done to promote artistic inquiry's acceptance and production?

I will address these three questions as they relate directly to dance/movement therapy and therapists. To illustrate the discussion about the evaluation of artistic inquiry, *Still/Here* will be revisited and assessed as to its effectiveness and potential value to the profession. The third question will be answered in the form of recommendations for further research and innovations that can be made within the field of dance/movement therapy.

WHEN IS IT APPROPRIATE TO USE ARTISTIC METHODS OF INQUIRY?

Corrine Glesne, whose work was discussed in Chapter 3, has answered this question regarding poetic transcription, the particular kind of artistic inquiry she has published.

> "When," I have been asked, "is poetic transcription appropriate and when should narrative transcription be used?" One could also inquire as to the appropriate instances to use readers' theatre, a short story, ethno-photography, or dance. My answer is, "it depends." It depends on the inclination of the presenter, the nature of the data, the intended purpose for writing up one's research, and the intended audience . . . . Researchers need to be aware of many ways to re-present data and to experiment with them to learn about their data, themselves in relation to the data, and about their skills and abilities to communicate inquiry in different ways. (Glesne, 1997, pp. 218-219)

I agree with Glesne and understand her answer as pointing toward four determining factors in considering artistic methods of research: the researcher, the data, the purpose, and the audience. I will expand on all four, but begin with the declaration that my bias is toward the importance of the first, the researcher.

THE RESEARCHER. As I have mentioned elsewhere, one of my main concerns is with the authentic representation of the work done by dance/movement therapists. When deliberating what kind of research to do, the dance/movement therapist should first and foremost recognize not simply what she or he is able to do, but in which research skills she or he excels. What is it that she can see that her colleagues may not even know exists? What can he describe with accuracy that others can barely see? How does he come to understand what he sees? In what forms can she communicate what she has found, that others would be unable to create? What tools does he uniquely wield? What stories, images, truths can she tell that few others have the privilege to witness?

When dance/movement therapists choose tools with which they are only minimally adept, they risk presenting themselves as inept. When they use languages in which they are not fluent, they come across as inarticulate. If dance/movement therapists see themselves as having no choice, and believe that traditional quantitative methods are the only viable ways to do research, then they need to devote extensive effort to become skilled in that modality in order to be perceived as competent professionals. But why not utilize the skills that so many dance/movement therapists have already worked hard to develop? If these skills are artistic, creative, or aesthetic, then artistic inquiry should be the method of choice.

THE DATA. The nature of the data very often dictates what tools need to be used to identify, observe, gather, organize, and understand. The wrong tool can completely miss the data in question. For instance, sound cannot be measured with a photometer. More to the point, the content of dreams cannot be shown on a galvanic skin response meter. The color of emotional pain cannot be expressed on a multiple-choice test. Interpersonal love cannot be felt with anything but what we call the human heart. The use of the most sensitive tool to accurately gather the desired data is of critical importance. In artistic inquiry, as in most forms of qualitative research, the primary data collection and analysis tool is the human being, who is highly trained to perceive and understand sensation, affect, and other subtle inter- and intrapersonal information.

All data come from a source and are embedded in a context. In dance/movement therapy, the source is a human being, and the context is that human being's life. Therefore, all comparisons to data gathered through scientific methods from inanimate sources that can be isolated or controlled are for the most part irrelevant. If the data is embedded in a context that cannot be manipulated without altering the essential nature of the experience and the information it yields, then some form of qualitative inquiry, including artistic inquiry, would be best suited. If the data cannot be quantified without changing its essential qualities, then again, a qualitative approach would be most appropriate.

When gathering data about the experiences of humans, methods developed for observing the behavior of animals who cannot communicate are also unsuitable. The ethical study of humans occurs in the realm of dialogue and relationship in which cooperative inquiry is a natural component. When faced with the (at times) willfully inaccessible intrapsychic lives of human beings, science, which has mastered the observable, is faced with serious problems. Questions about the inner realm of human beingness very often lead to emotional and intuitive data that is expressed through stories, symbols, images, postural changes, gestures, inarticulate sounds: in other words, the raw materials of the arts. The creative arts therapies specialize in the transformation of this kind of data into artistic forms that lead to successful communication of profound inner experiences from one human being to another. If the research question is about these inner experiences of clients and therapists, and if the resulting data is rich in emotional, intuitive, or imaginal content, then artistic inquiry that can transform this data into communicable form without losing its essential meaning is the best approach.

THE PURPOSE. I return to the assumption stated in Chapter 1 that the primary purpose of any research is the drive toward a *fuller, deeper, more accurate* understanding of something that is important to the researcher. Inherent in this assumption are three dimensions of understanding identified as fullness, depth, and accuracy.

The dimension of fullness suggests a qualitative *filling out* with richness of detail, a thorough *filling in* of empty places in the realm of the research question, and a *filling up* that satisfies the curiosity of the researcher.

What qualitative details are best *filled out* by art? The norm for the presentation of findings in today's psychological research is the statistical result. The numerical information is often transposed onto a graph for easier comprehension. Numbers and graphs provide abstract quantitative detail, but do not attempt to fill out sensory detail. Even more obvious is the fact that this information is disembodied. It cannot reflect the bodies of either the researcher/clinician or her clients. Statistical representation of dance/movement therapy is like an anorexic woman denying and defying her own flesh. If dance/movement therapy is in fact the unique hybrid of dance and the human sciences that it seems to be, then at least some of its research needs to be embodied, kinesthetic, and sensory. If essential meaning uncovered by the inquiry cannot be starved into numerical form, or the researcher feels that the sensory evidence is essential to the findings, then artistic methods of presentation would be best suited to fill out the sensory, embodied details.

What places are not *filled in*, but left empty by traditional forms of research? One of the spaces into which neither empirical nor numerical data can lead is the realm of intuitive knowing. Intuition needs neither fact nor logic to reach conclusions that are none-the-less recognized as true. We know that intuitive insight is frequently a critical step in the development of scientific research, but it cannot be acknowledged in the scientific method. Artistic inquiry makes a place for this kind of knowing and can therefore fill in the intuitive gaps left by scientific methodology. Artistic methods are largely intuitive and can therefore, be used to describe the methodology rather than leave aspects of it invisible or unspoken.

What curiosity is *filled up*, or satisfied by artistic methods? The ability to satisfy depends on the nature of the need or the desire. Curiosity is the desire to know, and as has been discussed in Chapter 1, there are many kinds of knowing. If the researcher has a desire to know logically; abstractly; mathematically; or with absolute, predictable, statistical certainty, then the scientific method will satisfy this curiosity. However, if the researcher wants to know emotionally, intersubjectively, intuitively, aesthetically, spatially, kinesthetically, musically, or spiritually, then the scientific method will not satisfy his or her curiosity. Only a qualitative or artistic inquiry will satisfy these desires.

The dimension of understanding called depth in the description of the purpose of research implies a more profound understanding that pushes below the surface of appearances. I refer again to the metaphor of how quantitative research seems to present a box with a label on it that refers to what is inside, but does not allow us to open it up and experience it. Artistic inquiry invites us into the experiential depths of the box. Elliott Eisner (1991) saw the differences between scientific and artistic research in similar terms. He distinguished between the way that science "states meaning" and art "expresses" it by turning to John Dewey and Suzanne Langer for clarification. He quoted Dewey's explanation that science, at its most effective "sets forth the conditions under which an experience of an object or situation may be had. . . . They can be used as directions by which we may arrive at the experience." (In the box metaphor, this would be like pasting directions about how to open a box on the outside of one like it.) Art, in contrast "does something different from leading to an experience. It constitutes one" (p. 31). Similarly, Langer described representational symbols (used in science) as pointing toward the meanings they attempt to convey, whereas presentational symbols (used in art) recreate qualities of the expressed meaning so that they may be experienced directly. If the information that the researcher has discovered would be best understood by others through the kind of depth experience that Langer and Dewey claimed art enables, rather than simply by rational, discursive reference to it; and if the researcher believes that the consumers and critics are willing and able to enter into the experience, then artistic inquiry would be the method of choice.

Accuracy is a dimension of understanding most often claimed by scientific methods rather than by artistic. Accuracy sometimes means exact conformity in the reproduction of a perceived version of reality. In dance/movement therapy, only a strictly representational method, such as a live or videotaped exact reproduction of movement would satisfy this requirement of accuracy. But the more the data is artistically interpreted, the less this kind of accuracy is present. Accuracy can also refer to the representation of truth rather than error. This recalls the discussions of truth in Chapters 1 and 3 in which it was suggested that depending on what one's understanding of truth is, artistic methods can and do convey truth. Accuracy also suggests authenticity or honesty of representation, and this meaning speaks to my concerns regarding the accurate representation of dance/movement therapists' values, epistemologies, and methods as researchers. If the prospective researcher has concerns about presenting himself or herself with this kind of accuracy, then artistic inquiry might best address these concerns.

There are other purposes for doing research, which some may consider more important than the desire to understand dance/movement therapy, therapists and their clients more fully, deeply, and accurately. These include the desire for professional recognition in the form of job security (tenure for instance), more dance/movement therapy jobs, medical insurance reimbursement for dance/movement therapy services, and legislation providing licensure and guaranteeing the right to practice. Admittedly, if outcome and efficacy studies are the only kind of research that a potential researcher sees as serving these purposes, then the choice to do more traditional quantitative studies seems obvious. Nevertheless, I believe it is possible that these organizational systems from which the profession wants recognition can be reached with artistic inquiry projects. Some possibilities will be proposed in the upcoming recommendations section.

THE AUDIENCE. In theater and dance, the concept of audience

embraces the producers, critics, theater owners, funding foundations, the artistic community made up of colleagues and competitors, and members of the public who directly and indirectly consume and form opinions of the production. Broadly speaking, the audience is the market for the production. Although the "audience" is never simply those who fill the house, the bottom line for success or failure is none-the-less whether the house is full. Theoretically, this is true for research as well.

In dance/movement therapy, I think it is not too risky to suggest that the consumers of research in dance/movement therapy are primarily other dance/movement therapists, and a small proportion of them at that. Research in dance/movement therapy is almost exclusively published in the *American Journal of Dance Therapy*, which is currently struggling to find articles to publish. Occasionally *The Arts in Psychotherapy* will publish research done in dance/movement therapy, which means that other creative arts therapists do jury and read it. Dance/movement therapy research is rarely found in the journals of allied professions such as occupational and recreational therapies or various psychotherapies. At the annual conferences of The American Dance Therapy Association, research presentations and poster sessions are attended by a small percentage of the portion of the professional body that attends the conference.

My point is that research of any sort in dance/movement therapy barely has an audience. Research in dance/movement therapy is basically not filling the house, and options for future productions are very slim. If it wants an audience, it is going to have to create one. Based on the primary goal of research being greater understanding of what is important to the researcher(s), it makes sense to begin with dance/movement therapists as the audience and find out what they want and need to know. When a way is found to sufficiently excite them about doing and consuming research, then find out who else they want to excite, motivate, and move with their findings. But unless there is an internal source of energy and motivation that dance/movement therapists can convey, and a vision that they can stand behind and give form to, efforts to sell dance/movement therapy to others are going to be unimpressive. If the profession can produce research that is vibrant, powerful, meaningful, and communicates the essence of dance/movement therapy, finding a producer and filling the house will become easier.

HOW CAN ARTISTIC INQUIRY BE EVALUATED?

Artistic inquiry differs from other forms of research in the ways that have been explicated in Chapters 3 through 5. To review, it may use artmaking to gather and analyze data and may present its findings in an artistic form. It may proceed creatively, evolving methodological innovations rather than following a predetermined scientific method. The artistic researcher may rely on his or her aesthetic motivation and judgment to determine the paths and forms the research will take. In these ways, artistic inquiry is like art and can only be evaluated the way art is—aesthetically.

However, artistic inquiry is also similar to other forms of research in several ways: the researcher identifies a research question; explicates a methodology; is responsible for the ethical treatment of participants; and must work toward the usefulness of the findings. In these areas, artistic inquiry may be evaluated in the same ways works of qualitative inquiry are. Thus, a synthesis of criteria, some drawn from the field of research and some from the field of aesthetics, will be needed for comprehensive evaluation of artistic inquiry projects.

Evaluation essentially means to determine the value. The questions then arise: Value to whom? And who is doing the evaluating? I will answer both questions myself, as a dance/movement therapist, educator, and researcher in an effort to explicate the idea of value. When does research have value to me? The answer is really very simple: when I understand it and when it is useful to me. The first part of the answer is about effectiveness of communication on the part of the research and about my ability to perceive and understand it. The second, usefulness, is about either practical application of the findings or enhanced theoretical understanding of the subject.

If I answer the original questions differently, say from the perspective of the editors of a professional journal or curator of a nontraditional venue of presentation, effectiveness of communication and usefulness are still crucial. However, usefulness has a different perspective, in that these venues are concerned with what will appeal to their audiences and address their missions.

Clearly, the inquiry has value to the artist/researcher as well, making him or her the first evaluator. Thus, the researcher exercises evaluative judgment throughout, based on his or her aesthetic, scholarly, and professional values. (This initial evaluative process has been discussed in regard to aesthetic determination and art-making.) Yet in the creative process that is research at several subsequent points the product is offered to others for feedback, acceptance, or unfortunately, rejection. One such time is the proposal stage, another is submission to the gatekeepers of publication or presentation venues, and the final stage is the presentation to the public/audience. At each of these stages, evaluation may be either aesthetic or more traditional, and the foci of the evaluations will vary.

The stage during which the research question is examined most critically is when it is proposed to an academic committee or sponsoring organization. Even in artistic inquiry, the proposal is most apt to be submitted in written form, though in my experience, committees are often happy to have the proposal supplemented with artistic presentations. Members of these committees will decide if it has value to future researchers, to the profession as a whole, to people served by the profession, and to stakeholders who might support the research financially. Proposal evaluators are likely to represent a variety of disciplines and may not be aesthetically conscious. Therefore, interdisciplinary language with which the artist/researcher can clearly articulate the question, purpose, and the methodology will be most valuable.

At this stage, artistic inquiry can be evaluated much like any other research proposal, except that it may not describe a familiar methodology. It is the responsibility of the proposal's author to communicate his or her vision of the process and the product, which may require some creative writing skills. Needless to say, the intentions of the inquiry must be delineated with as much detail as possible. The creative process of the researcher needs to be anticipated, with some indication of where the form may take unexpected turns depending on the unfoldment of the data and its meaning. It is the responsibility of the evaluator to challenge the researcher to articulate ideas that may not be explicit enough if they are still known only tacitly. If this dialogue can occur respectfully and with flexibility from both parties, the nature of the inquiry should become discernible.

Once the methodology is discerned, the evaluators must determine if it will be safe for all involved, if the rights of all participants will be respected throughout the inquiry, and if plans for informed consent are in place. Because artistic inquiry may involve innovative processes, ethical issues may surface in new ways and be more difficult to recognize. Later in this chapter, the discussion about the interface of ethics and aesthetics in the evaluation of Jones' *Still/Here* will illustrate this possibility.

The proposal evaluators also assess if the inquiry holds the promise of new and useful information. Even if the research topic is one that has been previously addressed, the unique approaches possible in artistic inquiry may result in new perspectives. Ideally, evaluators also consider whether the proposed methods maximize the artist/researcher's skills and offer an authentic representation of their work in dance/movement therapy.

Once the research is completed, it is submitted to a venue for presentation or publication. Depending on the venue, the evaluative criteria will differ tremendously. For instance, if it takes written, scholarly form and is submitted for publication to a professional journal with a traditional format, then the usual assessments of grammar, punctuation, word usage, clarity of expression, organization of ideas, and so forth, will be appropriate. Once the effectiveness of the communication is determined, then the findings will be assessed as to their value to the profession and to the mission of the journal. If the editors do not recognize the described methodology, or if they are looking for more familiar forms of research, then the researcher may simply need to submit the article elsewhere. If the editors are open to, but inexperienced with, aesthetic critique and the idea of research as a creative process, it might be best if their efforts were focused on evaluating the aspects of the inquiry that are most like traditional research. To evaluate the aesthetic qualities of the product and the creative process of the inquiry, guest editors who have experience in arts-based research might be invited to collaborate with the inexperienced editors.

For art to be considered research by those who are responsible for its evaluation, it must engage in some kind of systematic process that the artist/researcher can describe, although it need not adhere to a predetermined or standardized system. What distinguishes it as systematic is the intentional recognition of the process in relation to the question. The method needs to have internal consistency, and if it veers creatively from a consistent method, the researcher needs to be able to identify the irregularities and a rationale for them. I believe this can be done without quelling creative, aesthetic, and artistic motivations or actions. It does require the researcher to bring a heightened awareness to the creative and artistic processes that were used, thereby supporting an articulate description of them. For example, in *Still/Here* the presentation was purely artistic, and the methodology was not explicated at all until other supporting documentation was released. Until that point, it was clearly art, but after the explication of the methodology, it could easily be perceived as research as well. If it is the goal of the artist/researcher to present the inquiry as research, then the methodology needs to be described clearly. This does not mean that it is necessarily presented in the standard scholarly form used in most professional journals. It could take any form that illustrates the systematic (including creative or artistic) process of gathering and analyzing data and shaping the presentation of findings.

If the inquiry is submitted to a very different kind of venue, such as a theater or a gallery, aesthetic criteria may be the primary considerations for determining its value and effectiveness. For instance, dancer and educational researcher Blumenfeld-Jones identified one of the bases for his evaluation in an article about dance as research. Regarding dance as a medium to present findings, he said "the quality of the dance must be made paramount, which means design and execution must be excellent" (1995, p. 400). In a theatrical context, certainly the quality of the choreography and performance will determine its ability to communicate its intended meaning to its audience and will add to its value to producers and sponsors. Many dance/movement therapists are not accustomed to thinking about choreography and performance as part of their practice, but many are none-the-less skilled in both or have been at times in their careers. I believe the idea of combining these aesthetic skills with clinical ones is at the heart of dance/movement therapy, though it may not be at the fore of its current professional identity or consciousness. For artistic inquiry to find presentational venues, these aesthetic values will need to be reinvited into the communal consciousness and applied to the creation and evaluation of projects that use artistic research methods.

Once the effectiveness of a particular inquiry to communicate to the intended audience has been established, then its usefulness to that audience must be questioned. Those who know the audience best would be best qualified for this task. This would be relatively easy for dance/movement therapists to assess about themselves as the audience for a journal article or a conference workshop, but what about presentational situations in which the audience is not comprised exclusively of dance/movement therapists? The responsibility seems to lie with the researchers to know their intended audiences well and to know what information and presentational form they will find not just useful but also evocative, inspiring, disturbing, or motivating. For instance, dance/movement therapists may think they know what hospital administrators would find useful, but perhaps they should consider what might disturb, inspire, or provoke them into deeper reflection or action.

If the methodology and the findings are expressed in artistic form, it might behoove the artist/researcher to accompany them with a brief verbal description of the motivating questions and the methodology. This could be a spoken introduction, a written abstract, program notes, or what is sometimes called a contextual essay. Although this suggestion may seem to contradict the claim for the communicative powers of art, I believe the presence of such a statement will serve to orient the audience and increase the likelihood of their appreciation for the artistic aspects of the work.

One real possibility is that the aesthetic values of researchers and evaluators may clash, especially if the inquiry uses innovative processes and presentational mediums. In these cases, it may be necessary to develop alternative venues for presentation unless or until changes can be made within the already existing ones. Recommendations for what venues might be explored will be made later in this chapter.

EVALUATING *STILL/HERE* AS A WORK OF ARTISTIC INQUIRY

In this section, *Still/Here* will be used as an illustration to help ground some of these evaluative concerns in an example that I think will help enhance an understanding of artistic inquiry's potential. In returning to Jones' work, I invite readers to imagine how they might approach the task of assessing its effectiveness and usefulness to the profession if its creator were a dance/movement therapist. This invitation will be in the form of questions, most of which cannot be answered by readers who have not seen *Still/Here* themselves. I leave many unanswered because they are intended to be applicable to *any* work of artistic inquiry and to be provocative to thought about research in dance/movement therapy.

Was this inquiry of value to the intended audience? Jones' audience was the general public and the art/dance community within which he works. There can be no question that living with a life-threatening illness is a phenomenon with timeless existential significance to almost anyone. There are those, like *New York Times* columnist Frank Rich, who have said that it is especially meaningful now. In response to *Still/Here*, Rich wrote "AIDS is responsible for yanking death out of the American closet . . . . This is the story of our time" (Duffy, 1995, p. 69). Living with the possibility of imminent death is an uncomfortable thing to imagine, and that discomfort keeps most people from getting close enough to know more, unless they are brought closer by illness itself. As one Survival Workshop participant said: "The questions that people who face a serious illness have are questions that all thoughtful adults have but just don't think about" (Jones, 1995, p. 265). Along those same lines, dance critic and academician Marcia Siegel commented on Jones' work, "If there is such a thing as victim art, I think its purpose is to shock us, to arrest our complacency about human catastrophe" (1996, p. 62). What value might arousal from complacency have for dance/movement therapists or for, let's say, administrators of health insurance companies?

Did this particular method effectively communicate new understanding in a unique and valuable way that other methods could not? After viewing the version of *Still/Here* adapted to video by Bender and Jones (1996) I was left with some questions about its ability to stand alone, without the supportive background material available through Moyers' video, Jones' book, and the various talks I have had the opportunity to hear. It may be that the dance by itself communicates only a small part of the whole story that with the other supporting resources is made so full, accessible, and alive. But isn't this the case with any research? It can only be a partial telling, and is limited by the form it takes, whether it is a conference presentation, poster session, journal article, theater piece, or poem. Every additional presentation method or medium used serves to expand our understanding of the discovery. The addition of the other forms of documentation also made *Still/Here* more like a work of research, in that they revealed Jones' intentions and methods. It is worth considering the necessity of these supporting resources being available to increase the practical application of this kind of inquiry. What audiences for artistic inquiry in dance/movement therapy would need more contextual data?

Would dance/movement therapists be likely to receive fuller, deeper, or more accurate understanding from *Still/Here* without additional information? Compared to almost any other audience, dance/movement therapists would probably be most likely to understand. Does *Still/Here*, without the additional documentation, contribute *uniquely* to the understanding of people coping with life-threatening illness? I think it does. I refer to a quote by Shaun McNiff that describes for me what *Still/Here* accomplished:

> Human events are generally characterized by vastly complex, interdependent elements which work together or against one another within a world structure of constant movement. Great art works participate in the event itself and embody the complexity, empirically, with forms that enable people to grasp multiplicity while also experiencing the aesthetic coherence of the artwork. (McNiff, 1986, p. 283)

What *Still/Here* communicates through its multiple mediums of expression are the complex, many-layered, phenomenological qualities of the experience. For instance, as a work of art it says more to me than could be said with words arranged in a linear, predetermined, traditional form about the *quality of aloneness* one experiences in the particular life passage it explored. The aloneness was colored and textured by a variety of emotional states, from sexual to numbing. The aloneness was accompanied and witnessed, yet untouched by the bodies and actions of other people, no matter how physically close they may have been. The aloneness ran deep as each dancer moved alongside others who were also dancing their struggle. The inescapable nature of this aloneness seemed to drive the characters in the dance toward a Higher Power and toward a passage through life's final door.

These were the understandings that *Still/Here* offered me, but *simultaneously* it spoke of many other things, and on many other levels of consciousness. To others it revealed other things. At another time it might reveal a different understanding to me. McNiff described this phenomenon:

> What the picture offers depends upon the person's ability to see and receive its expression. Past experience and personal preoccupations will effect what is seen, but these are elements within a dialogue between image and view-

er. Like any other relationship, the interaction will be distinguished by its unique entanglements. Although formal qualities in paintings will often stimulate "identical factors" in perceivers (Arnheim, p. 449 [Art and visual perception, University of California Press, Los Angeles, CA, 1954]), the image will also elicit different responses. (1993, p. 5)

What might dance/movement therapists and those they wish to inform bring to a viewing of *Still/Here* that would influence what they saw? For most therapists working with this population, quality of life in survival (rather than cure) is the goal of therapy. Would these therapists see insights into quality of life revealed in the dance? Could someone with cost effectiveness and quickly attainable therapeutic outcomes as primary concerns be moved by the stories told in the dance? Is *Still/Here* accessible enough to nondancers to effectively communicate its message to them as well as to those trained to see meaning in movement?

In the way art can simultaneously reveal diverse individual truths as well as reflections of universal experience, *Still/Here* opened a world of possible ways to perceive the soul's experience of life nearing death in a manner similar to what James Hillman described:

> The soul is ceaselessly talking about itself in ever recurring motifs, in ever-new variations, like music; . . . this soul is immeasurably deep and can only be illumined by insights, flashes in a vast cavern of incomprehension, and that in the realm of the soul, the ego is a paltry thing. (In McNiff, 1987, p. 291)

Jones, through his outer dialogue with survivors, succeeded in illuminating the soul's inner dialogue in *Still/Here*, and I feel confident in saying that he could not have done so without the use of an artistic inquiry. For whom might the illumination of the souls of dance/movement therapy clients have value? Who might it inspire, motivate, provoke toward action?

Did *Still/Here* authentically employ Jones' skills and resources while maximizing their usefulness *and* his integrity as an inquirer? I also think it did this. I believe Jones was acting as fully and as authentically an artist and human being as he could at that moment in his career, perhaps heightened by this heuristic quest for greater spiritual understanding. As he said to Bill Moyers, "I want to find out what this point in my life means. . . . You know how the old song goes, 'Lord I want to be ready'? I see this as getting ready." (1997). Art was his purpose, his form, but he allowed it to be a clear inquiry into sources beyond his imaginings, beyond himself. Could a dance/movement therapist have done something similar? Could a work similar to *Still/Here*, but on a smaller scale, such as a conference presentation, be effective and useful?

Are there conflicts between ethical and aesthetic motivations in *Still/Here*? Revisiting the central question that Arlene Croce (1994) raised about *Still/Here* as victim art: Could one's own compassion for the real people involved interfere with one's ability and right to evaluate the work? This holds particular relevance for research in dance/movement therapy, in which clinicians witness and research emotional pain more often than not. To clarify this point, an audience may not have trouble separating emotion from aesthetic judgment in a fictional account. However, if the artist were sharing his or her own real-life tragedy, the evaluators might become caught in their own sympathy for the artist and be unable to exercise clarity in their aesthetic judgment. Asked simply, will evaluators feel pity for the struggles of the real artist/survivor and be unable to critique his or her work? These questions apply to research if it becomes difficult to assess the value of the research because of the power of the realities evoked by its authors, especially if, as in heuristic research, the authors are those who have suffered. Does anyone dare aesthetically criticize another who is perceived as having suffered enough already or as being damaged from his or her experiences?

This dilemma is resolved by the fact that the effectiveness of the artistic form (including the methodology and composition) is determined by how successfully it conveys the qualitative experience, including the emotions of the participants, while still maintaining its integrity as a whole (Eisner, 1991; Lawrence-Lightfoot & Davis, 1997). If the goal of artistic inquiry is to create a form of research that communicates as art does, then emotional responses are an indispensable part of the package.

This resolution is acceptable if the artist/performer/researcher is the victim or survivor and chooses intentionally to present and subject his or her experience to aesthetic scrutiny. But what if the artist/inquirer/clinician presents the suffering of another who might have possibly suffered in the process of disclosure? The ethical question provoked by the use of victims/survivors and their stories in art or in research is whether it is right for the artistic researcher to use the work (in this case emotional work) of another as means to her or his own ends. Was Jones using the emotional riches of his workshop participants to line his own pockets? Does one ever have the right to use anyone else's story to address her or his own needs? Certainly these are questions to be alert to, but in the case of *Still/Here* and the Survival Workshops, if all accounts are accurate, Jones made his plans and purposes very clear to the people with whom he worked. In research terms, all participated with informed consent. If, knowing how their emotional work was to be used, participants consented to share themselves and their stories, then this does not seem to be unethical use. Additionally, if participants agreed to have their images, movements, and words transformed into "art", then they accepted exposure to the public, including critics who assess the aesthetic value of the work. How would the professional body of dance/movement therapy view a clinician who used the stories and therapeutic work of her or his clients to construct a work of art? Would the arguments used in this paragraph reassure a research ethics committee that all participants were safe and understood the nature of the inquiry and its results?

RECOMMENDATIONS

The following recommendations are for the purpose of increasing the acceptance of artistic inquiry among dance/movement therapists and furthering the likelihood of projects being produced and shared through publication or presentation. In this section I will be writing as I did at times in the Introduction, as one member of the body of professional dance/movement therapists and will therefore be referring to myself and my colleagues in the first person plural. I simply feel more comfortable making suggestions to the profession while acknowledging my own place within it.

First and foremost, I believe it is essential that we maintain a strong connection with our personal and communal dance identities, not only to encourage artistic inquiry, but to insure the continuation of the practice of dance/movement therapy. This could be supported by the requirement of dance classes as part of graduate training and continuing education. Attending dance performances could likewise be required or rewarded. Conferences could provide ideal opportunities to share our dance skills with our colleagues through performances or dance-oriented workshops. Regional and national publications could be forums for autobiographical essays about how clinicians integrate their dance identities and experiences with their dance/movement therapy work.

Related to this is the importance of developing our individual and collective aesthetic consciousness in relation to the practice of dance/movement therapy. Scholarly and informal discussions about the aesthetics of dance/movement therapy initiated through existing publications, various collegial electronic networks, classrooms, and conference presentations could stimulate thought about the place of aesthetics in clinical practice as well as research. Aesthetic values, such as those I suggested in Chapter 5, could be brought to consciousness as part of the graduate dance/movement therapy curriculum. Learning or strengthening skills in other art forms as well could enrich the aesthetic sensibilities of individual dance/movement therapists.

It is important here to clarify that I am not advocating that dance/movement therapists begin experimenting with art forms about which they are curious to produce interesting variations on the research theme. I am recommending that we use our most highly developed artistic skills to create artistic inquiry of the best possible quality.

General appreciation of our dance identity and aesthetic values will lay the foundation for an open attitude toward the idea of artistic inquiry. It will also increase the likelihood of editorial boards and conference committees feeling competent to assess the value of artistic inquiry projects submitted for publication or presentation. However, specific education about artistic inquiry as a viable methodology will need to occur both at the graduate and postgraduate levels. I very strongly believe that graduate research courses need to be taught by dance/movement therapists and that the course needs to be aimed toward the research skills that are specific to dance/movement therapists in training. Generic research courses create confusion as to the professional identity of the students and mislead them into perceiving research as something that must be done the way social workers or psychologists do it. Dance/movement therapists who have already been educated about research in this limited way can be reeducated at conferences as to the artistic options available.

Further research to support the argument for doing artistic inquiry would be a large scale assessment of the epistemologies of dance/movement therapists. Testing based on Howard Gardner's Theory of Multiple Intelligences would be ideal for this purpose. It might also be useful to document more about what dance/movement therapists perceive as barriers to doing research.

To encourage the production of artistic inquiry, existing forums will need to open to its publication or presentation. At this point, the primary literary forum is the *American Journal of Dance Therapy (AJDT)*. Other professional journals such as *The Arts in Psychotherapy and Qualitative Inquiry* have already invited artistic inquiry projects, and will draw them away from the *AJDT* if it is not proactive in soliciting artistic inquiry from dance/movement therapists. Editorial boards may need to be educated or expanded to include members who are willing and equipped to evaluate artistic inquiry projects. The other primary forum for research in dance/movement therapy is the Annual American Dance Therapy Association (ADTA) Conference, which would be an ideal place to showcase new and innovative forms of inquiry. Alternatives to poster sessions could be offered in the form of galleries for visual artworks, poetry readings, reader's theater, and most importantly, stages for artistic inquiry in the form of dance presentations. Workshops describing methodologies that have been and could be used would be informative and inspiring. Program committees would need to be educated or encouraged by the membership as to the value of such innovations.

Beyond existing forums, new ones will need to be developed to handle the diverse forms of much of artistic inquiry. Creative possibilities include multimedia electronic journals on the world wide web. These could present videotaped dances, visual art works, or music, which could all be accompanied by textual support materials. Video productions are another possibility that could be relatively simply disseminated to graduate programs; regional or national ADTA meetings; and conferences, program administrators, insurance company policy makers, and so forth. Public performances of artistic inquiry could be presented at undergraduate and graduate schools, the conferences of various professional bodies, and local venues used for other kinds of performances. Galleries could be approached for the use of their space to display visual arts as well as dance works. Private performances of multimedia or dance works could be given in almost any location, and invitations sent to people who are perceived as being decision makers around policy that impacts dance/movement therapy.

A possibility that I think has great potential is collaboration with recently developing community-based organizations that advocate for the use of the arts in supporting mental health (or survival from trauma for instance). Some of these are very active in hosting conferences, performances, and web sites.

As a final recommendation, I believe the best change that the profession could facilitate to encourage inquiry of any kind would be a profound and ubiquitous shift in attitude about research away from anxiety, doubt, and boredom toward hope, confidence, and excitement. All the suggestions that I have made in this conclusion are aimed at supporting that shift in consciousness.

CONCLUSION

To finish this discussion I would like to step back from the particular applications of artistic inquiry to research in dance/movement therapy for a moment and view again the larger picture of interdisciplinary research. There is a greater purpose that research like artistic inquiry is serving, and that purpose is just as urgent in dance/movement therapy as it is any discipline. Corrine Glesne suggested that:

> Experimental form seems to be demanding our attention as a way to help fill holes in our fragmented society. . . . In the process of blurring boundaries, experimental writing helps to heal wounds of scientific categorization and technological dehumanization. With its aesthetic sensibilities, experimental writing can introduce spirit, imagination, and hope. We struggle how to care for the soul (Moore, 1992 [Care of the soul, Harper-Perennial, New York]) in a world that has valued expert-led effectiveness, efficient time use (Just Do It), and materialism rather than creativity, reflection, and connection. (Glesne, 1997, pp. 214-215)

When dance/movement therapists identify more strongly with science than with art and value scientific ways of knowing above all others, there is serious danger of becoming fragmented and dehumanized. I believe many dance/movement therapists know this and many more feel it intuitively. Several years before Glesne, two pioneers in qualitative research made a pertinent observation: "Many, including scientists, are searching to find some spiritual core in themselves, a way of reconnecting to meaning, purpose, and the sense of wholeness and holiness" (Lincoln & Denzin, 1994, p. 582). I believe it is crucial for dance/movement therapy to remain connected to its spiritual core, its meaning, its reason for being uniquely what it is, to be a viable, thriving profession. It is my deepest hope that artistic inquiry will contribute to its vitality and longevity.

In closing, I offer the words of Walter Sorrell, infamous dance critic and author, as a final perspective on the value of artistic inquiry:

> Man suspects that there must be harmony in all chaotic complexity, there must be some reason for his own existence and some final answer to all questions. In his search for the secret he has found the key in art. It may not fit the last lock or open the ultimate gate; but it makes him walk through a thousand little doors and, with each door he leaves behind, he feels as if he had come one step closer to finding the secret. (Sorrell, 1971, p. 17)

Appendix

IDENTIFYING DANCE/MOVEMENT THERAPY STUDENTS' FEELINGS AND ATTITUDES ABOUT DOING RESEARCH: A PRETEST AND PEDAGOGICAL TOOL

Lenore Wadsworth

January 16, 1997

ABSTRACT

This project informally identified, for pedagogical purposes, a small sample of dance/movement therapy students' attitudes and feelings about doing research, before taking a research course, through quantitative, qualitative, and artistic methods of inquiry. Students were asked to describe their present attitudes and feelings about doing research through three methods:

1. By assigning their feelings to a number from one to ten.

2. By drawing a very quick, spontaneous squiggle drawing.

3. By writing a short paragraph.

Results were then analyzed and shared in ways appropriate to the kinds of data gathered. The findings were used to determine teaching methods and demonstrate a variety of research styles.

INTRODUCTION

The purpose of this project was three-fold. The first was to give me (the primary researcher and instructor) an overview of my students' attitudes and feelings about research, which would then have a formative influence on the particular teaching methods used in the research course to better meet their learning needs. The second was to provide the students with an opportunity to express their feelings about research in anticipation (based on experience with previous students) that there would be some anxiety about it. The third was to give students an applied educational experience of several different research methods.

My assumptions upon designing this project were that dance/movement therapy students have attitudes and feelings about research and that expressing these is supportive to their learning and to my teaching. I also assumed that drawing and dancing are valid ways of communicating feelings and attitudes, as are words and rating scales, and that each of these methods provides a different perspective of intrinsically equal value.

The intended consumers of the results of this project at the time of the research were the students (herein also termed coresearchers, artists, or dancers when referring to them in those roles) of the class. No individual identities are disclosed in this description, and including it here in no way that I can discern compromises the coresearchers or the intended purpose of the project.

The theoretical frameworks guiding this project were those of experiential education, cooperative research (Reason, 1988), and artistic inquiry (McNiff, 1986, 1987, 1993). In accordance with these theoretical positions, it was hoped that coresearchers would learn about themselves and about research through active engagement in the application of concepts and materials to facilitate multiple and integrated ways of knowing.

Questions intended to be addressed in this project included:

- What are the attitudes and feelings of these dance/movement therapy students about doing research at this time?

- What do each of the kinds of data (visual, verbal, and numerical) have to offer toward fuller understanding of student attitudes and feelings?

- In what ways will this project be an effective (or ineffective) manner of introducing basic research concepts to the students?

- Will the methods make sense and have meaning for the students?

- Are the methods directed toward the appropriate level of previous knowledge?

- Will the experience be as effective for students who are not feeling anticipatory anxiety about a research course?

- By which findings will coresearchers feel most accurately represented?

The scope of this particular project did not go beyond a small sample of adult dance/movement therapy students in a small, private, New England graduate school. It was not intended to stimulate generalization to students beyond this sample, but was instead designed to increase understanding about this small group.

METHODOLOGY

This project incorporated a combination of artistic, qualitative, and quantitative data collection, analysis, and presentation methods within a philosophically qualitative and artistic research framework. It yielded descriptive data through a single, small sample assessment of dance/movement therapy students' attitudes. Because of the relationship between the coresearchers/students and myself (the researcher/course instructor), it seemed essential to maintain the highest level of mutual respect and participation among us, which is characteristic of a qualitative, action-oriented posture. Because of the short-term purposes of the study (assessment, analysis, and application within one class period) the following very brief assessment tools and analysis techniques seemed best suited.

The small ($n=15$) sample group of coresearchers was preselected by this being a mandatory course in the second year of the master's level dance/movement therapy program. They had no preknowledge that they would be asked to participate in this research project. They were informed that it was a small research project for educational purposes. Their contribution and active participation in the study was encouraged as much as possible as part of their class participation.

There may have been an incentive on coresearchers' parts to represent their attitudes toward research as more positive than they actually were, to present themselves positively to the instructor. This may have skewed the quantitative assessment in a positive direction, impacting the internal validity of the research.

Similarly, ethical considerations included the possibility that the coresearchers, in their student roles, would feel pressured to participate in the research project to receive positive course evaluations. Because this would be their intention regardless of the class activity, I saw this as an ever-present positive incentive to participate that was typical to this context. Because the purpose of the research was ultimately to benefit these student coresearchers by assisting me in teaching them more effectively, I saw no ethical conflict of purposes.

It might be assumed that there would be concerns among coresearchers regarding exposure of personal material (feelings and attitudes) to me this early in the course. This was relieved somewhat by the fact that I had all these students the previous year in a course that had required the sharing of personal material, and so we all knew each other well as a result. None-the-less, accommodations were made within the research design to allow students the room to refrain from sharing their artwork with the group and to only share their written responses with other students. Any student had the option not to participate in any aspect of the project at any time and to observe instead.

Class participation of this kind is typical of the experiential learning methods used throughout this educational institution. Students are therefore very familiar with being asked to actively take part in learning experiences, though they are not often identified as "research." As part of a research class, however, this would not be a surprising or unusual event.

Data was collected using three methods:

1. On a small piece of paper, with a marker provided by me, participants were asked to write a number from one to ten (one being completely positive, confident, relaxed, pleasantly stimulated; ten being totally negative, anxious, afraid, disgusted, or disinterested) describing their attitude toward doing research right now. These numbers were then anonymously submitted to me.

2. On a piece of paper, with one marker provided by me, coresearchers were asked to very quickly draw a nonrepresentational, squiggle-like drawing of their feelings about research at this moment. I directed them not to think about it, but to let whatever they were feeling in their body in response to the idea of research simply move out their arm and onto the paper. Artists retained their own pictures.

3. On a lined piece of paper provided by me, using their own pens or pencils, coresearchers were asked to write a maximum of three full sentences describing their attitudes and feelings toward research at this time. These descriptions were retained by their authors.

Data was analyzed and presented using different methods for each group of data:

1. The numerical data was gathered and tabulated by me by finding the mean, median, and mode. I drew a simple frequency distribution on the board and indicated the three measures of central tendency with differently colored chalk. I did this with no assistance from coresearchers while they were doing other forms of data analysis.

2. Seated in a circle, drawings were shared simultaneously within the large group as all artists held up their individual drawings. (Any artist could elect not to show her or his drawing. Before showing the drawings, all artists were asked to agree not to evaluate any drawings as to better or worse quality in any way.) They were asked to comment on the similarities they saw between drawings in terms of aesthetic qualities such a shape, line, intensity, use of space, and so forth. They were then instructed to form clusters of similar drawings, the only inclusive requirement being that each artist in the cluster must agree that all drawings belonged there. The clusters then worked together to describe the aesthetic commonalities of their responses and created a short dance that embodied those aesthetic qualities. The clusters performed their dances for the larger group, which verbally responded by

describing the qualities they perceived in the dance. This method provided multiple levels of feedback and reflection for the coresearchers, and many opportunities to refine and clarify the qualities they wanted to communicate.

3. The written descriptions of feelings and attitudes were read by their authors within the small groups. This textual data was compared and contrasted to the nonverbal data analyzed in the previous activities. The cluster discussion at this point moved beyond aesthetics and into feelings and attitudes. The learning from the artistic and textual analyses was synthesized in this process. One spokesperson selected by each group took notes and reported back the identified themes of responses to the larger group, which met again in a circle when all groups were done.

A structural limitation of this design that very much determined the methods used was the brief period of time in which it was carried out. The methodology turned out to be well suited to this context and with clear direction from me as to how long each segment could take, all aspects of it were completed in a 2.5 hour time period. The quickness of the experience, however, did limit the depth to which the student's feelings and attitudes could be explored.

DISCUSSION OF PROCESS

DATA COLLECTION. After having the purpose of the research briefly explained to them, all students in the class (15) agreed to participate. Throughout, there was only one incident that may have indicated that there was one student who chose not to participate in one aspect of the research experience. This will be described in the next paragraph.

With a minimal introduction outlining the purpose of the research and the option not to participate, we began with the numerical data. While writing down their numbers from 1 to 10, the coresearchers pointed out that with one being high and ten being low, the numbers were in the opposite order than their usual associations to them. This may have caused some confusion or dissonance in the responses that was not intended. After the small papers were folded and collected in a box, I counted them and discovered there were only 14. I asked if anyone had chosen not to respond, but none acknowledged this. One response was then either lost or not given, and I did not take the time to redo the collection. Therefore the numerical data was one less than $n=15$.

During the drawings, the atmosphere and interactions were informal. I handed out drawing paper (about 6"x 8") and passed around a bag of markers. They could choose the color marker they wanted, and comments were humorously made about the significance of the color chosen. I jokingly replied that there could be no statistical significance because we could not assign them a quantitative value, but that there might be meaning. They asked for no further explanations as to how to do the drawings other than those I gave, which were described in the methodology. They drew for about one minute.

I handed out lined paper and asked them to write a maximum of three complete sentences regarding their feelings and attitudes about research. There were several comments at this point, the first one questioning the need to write full sentences. At least one student would have preferred to make a list of words, but I insisted on sentences. Another asked what I meant by "research." This is when I chose to narrow the question to "doing" research rather than asking about research as a broader topic (including aspects such as consuming and evaluating research). This was an unanticipated response and has since helped me to clarify the focus and methodology of subsequent research projects. The writing took about five minutes at the most. The coresearchers retained their drawings and their written descriptions.

DATA ANALYSIS. The analysis of the visual data was truly cooperative. Showing the drawings all together had an air of excitement, like "show & tell." After directing them to notice which pictures reminded them of their own, they began to point to one another's drawings and acknowledge similarities. It became clear to everyone that there were in fact significant resemblances; some pictures seeming almost identical, as if they had been drawn by the same person. They then pointed out some similarities between other peoples' drawings (not just their own and another's) that had not yet been noticed by the artists themselves. Together we identified aloud what the aesthetic elements were that people were noticing in preparation for the next level of analysis. There were one or two drawings that did seem unique, so that finding similar descriptive elements was more challenging for the coresearchers. I assisted at this point by suggesting some aesthetic elements they had not yet considered, such as location on the page and intensity of line.

With instruction to do so, the coresearchers gathered into small clusters of like drawings. There were one or two artists who felt torn between two clusters, identifying with aesthetic elements of each. I asked the ambivalent artists to resolve this by looking at the collection of each cluster as a whole and noting which group they felt most identified with. They eventually joined a cluster and everyone seemed satisfied with their membership.

The clusters then began identifying together the aesthetic similarities of the pictures. This was a time of very focused attention and quiet consideration for the groups. I had to remind them once not to get into a discussion of meaning at this point, but to stay with the aesthetic or visual elements. Identifying these elements seemed to get easier for the coresearchers as the discussion progressed.

With direction to begin creating a dance that reflected the qualities they had identified, a wave of excitement began that rose in energy and volume as the dances were formed. Gestural demonstrations and movement improvisations blossomed around the room. Artists, now dancers, experimented with embodying their own and others' image ideas. This was their medium, and their creative, full-bodied involvement in it was wonderful to observe. After about ten minutes, the clusters had all completed short dances that they were ready to share with the large group.

Each dance was completely unique and did truly embody the elements of its inspirational drawings. Each group found a way to display the pictures for their performance. Two arranged the drawings on the wall behind them, like scenery. One put them on the floor in the center of their dance. The other arranged them in front of the observers on the floor. Some dances were primarily circular in their use of space, some more linear or chaotically distributed, but all used the space deliberately. Some were more structured than others, with choreographed movement patterns. Others used more improvised movement. All had clear beginnings, middles, and endings.

After each performance, the observers responded with single descriptive words that they felt captured the aesthetic qualities of the dance. I wrote these down on a flip chart for each dance. After the observers were done sharing their responses, I asked the dancers if we had missed anything, so that they could point out elements that either they had not successfully conveyed, or the observers had not been sensitive to. For the most part there were very few qualities that were not perceived and identified by the observers. The dancers seemed very satisfied with their products and their ability to communicate.

Once all the dances were performed, I asked each cluster to meet again for a few minutes to process the experience. I also asked them to begin to consider what the aesthetic qualities of their dances meant to them in regard to the content of the question (how they felt about doing research). This was the first time that meaning was addressed directly, and the discussions were lively for the five minutes I could allow them.

This segued into an analysis of the textual data. I asked each cluster member to read his or her written responses to the group to be followed by the cluster identifying themes among the readings. When clusters reported back to the larger group, it became clear that their discussion of the writings had been highly influenced by the previous artistic analysis, as coresearchers heard the themes that had been identified in the drawings and dances reflected in the writings. But it also illuminated how much processing of emotional material had been done during the artistic analysis, as many of the writings seemed to their authors to be reflections of the distant past, or in some cases, shallow compared to the depth with which they had been addressing the identified issues during the creative process.

Themes that arose that were particularly relevant to teaching research were anxiety, containment, strength of form, balance, ambivalence, boredom, and subjectivity of interpretation. Anxiety was identified in about half the drawings and dances as jagged edges or chaotic, fast, repetitive action. In all cases, however, the anxiety was contained on the page or in the designated dance space with varying amounts of space around it. As instructor and researcher I found myself hopefully identifying this and interpreting it (subjectively and to myself) as a sense of containment that the school, course, instructor, or research exercise were providing. This theme of containment or strength of form given in response to anxious or chaotic feelings was also present in a group of responses that clearly identified research as some kind of a linear process that made sense out of confusion.

In the drawings and dances, the anxiety was often balanced by complementary forms such as curves, spirals, and sustained lines or gestures. This contrast between angular, fast, bound, chaotic forms and flowing, circular, sustained ones illustrated contrasting feelings that were later identified as ambivalence about research.

The theme of boredom, or lack of interest, excitement or sufficient information about research was identified in a large group of drawings. A subtitle given this dance by a subgroup of its creators was "bad karma," reflecting previous bad experiences with research that had caused a shut down of interest and hope. Despite the negative content of their responses, they were actively engaged in the data collection and analysis processes.

The final theme that came up around the analysis rather than from any of the groups' artistic responsed was that of the subjective nature of the qualitative research process. I attempted to distinguish the somewhat more objective process of identifying visual characteristics like lines, shapes, colors, or textures within the data, from the more subjective process of making meaning, either by the artists themselves or by the observers. We acknowledged that either was still more interpretive than collecting and analyzing numbers. A very brief discussion ensued about the nature and value of qualitative data of this type.

What I appreciated most about this whole analysis of artistic and textual data was its active, collaborative nature. Everyone was fully involved in every step, from drawing, to clustering, to dancing, to identifying descriptors and themes. There was an enthusiasm and interest throughout. It was provocative and also a little magical in that most of the students had never considered finding meaning in this kind of data and had never considered this kind of activity research.

Finally, I presented the analysis of the numerical data. I drew a very basic histogram of the frequency distribution, which allowed us to see the configuration of the spread. Because the sample was so small, it was difficult to see much of a shape, but it seemed to be a slightly asymmetrical bimodal distribution, with responses clustered around three and seven/eight. I explained how to find the mean, median, and mode and identified the location of each on the histogram. I asked them which measure of central tendency best described this group's response and all agreed that the bimodal spread did.

QUESTIONS

I had identified seven questions that I hoped would be addressed in some part by this small research project.

1. What are the attitudes and feelings of these dance/movement therapy students about doing research at this time? As a result of three data analyses I would venture to say that the attitudes of this group vary widely from very positive to very negative, with almost no middle ground, and with a slightly heavier response on the negative end, indicated by the results of the numerical scale. The meaning of "positive" was elaborated in the discussion about the drawings and textual data, with "hopeful" and "excited" being most often identified. The meaning of "negative" was also revealed in the discussions to mean "bored," "hopeless," "uninformed", and "anxious." The analyses also revealed ambivalence represented in many of the drawings and dances, illustrating the same split of extreme feelings *within* many individuals. I found it interesting that the bimodal response was therefore representative of both individual and group mixed feelings.

2. What do each of the kinds of data (visual, verbal, and numerical) have to offer toward fuller understanding of student attitudes and feelings? As I have indicated earlier, the visual (drawings) and verbal (textual) data and their analyses were the richest sources of understanding as far as I was concerned. As an instructor, I heard the nature of their concerns and attitudes in much greater depth than I would have had I simply asked them aloud in class how they felt. I believe they heard themselves and each other with more depth and detail also. The drawing and dancing held their interest and involved them actively, revealing information that they didn't know was there, surprising them.

The textual data analysis was not as clearly executed as I would have liked it to be. I found it difficult to give them directions for an abbreviated and successful textual analysis that could be done in the time we had and with their level of experience. The coresearchers were also already saturated with the results of the visual analysis, and in many cases the textual data simply replicated or confirmed what they had already said and heard.

The numerical data resulted in a very concrete representation of the range of feelings/attitudes. I found myself curious to find out the results, even after we were saturated from the first two data analyses. This indicates to me that the numerical scores held some additional information that the drawing and textual data did not clearly reveal. Perhaps it is because each person had to commit to a single number, as if to say "After all is said and done, where do I ultimately stand?" It allowed no room for the ambivalent and ineffable responses that the other data did. It was simple and clear, although by itself revealed absolutely no information as to the meanings of the numbers people chose for themselves.

As a group, we discussed the differences between these three ways of representing how the group felt about doing research, and all agreed that they complemented each other; that each provided what another could not. We came up with the metaphor for the numerical data of a big cardboard packing box with a label that identifies what's inside but doesn't really describe it well enough to satisfy ones' curiosity. The numerical data clearly does not satisfy sensory and emotional queries. The drawing, dancing, and textual analysis provided "hands on," depth exploration of the data as a dynamic entity whose meaning evolved as the analysis did.

3. In what ways will this project be an effective (and ineffective) manner of introducing basic research concepts? In general, it felt like a very effective way to introduce research concepts and covered quite a comprehensive range of them in a very short time. The limits were more likely to be my own limits of knowledge (i.e., in response to questions about statistical analysis for instance) than limits of the method. Perhaps the textual and statistical portions of the analysis would have been just as rich as the artistic if I had an equal passion for numbers and words as I do for images and movement. Given more time, all the research concepts could have been addressed in more depth, right within the framework of the research project. It can potentially be revisited in future classes for further elaboration.

4. Will the methods make sense and have meaning for the students? Based on their active involvement, questions, and comments, the methods seemed to make sense and be meaningful for the students. The low point of sense making was during the statistical portion, and again this was most likely due to my own limits of understanding. Two aspects of the experience seemed especially meaningful: making the dances (because these people were dancers) and discovering the contrast between the three different kinds of data and how to deal with them.

5. Are the methods directed toward the appropriate level of previous knowledge? This is difficult to assess. I think there was a wide range of understanding and previous experience with research in the class. I would need to talk to individual students to see if it provided new understanding or awareness for all those with previous experience. It was notably difficult for one student during the numerical data analysis.

6. *Will the experience be as effective for students who are not feeling anticipatory anxiety about a research course?* This is a complex question. Those who are experiencing some anxiety (to a point) are more highly aroused and therefore more engaged in the learning process. There were a group of students whose style of coping with anxiety (as evidenced in their drawings, dances, and their own interpretations) was to feel bored or hopeless rather than anxious. Surprisingly, these students seemed to be as actively engaged in the learning process as the anxious students for most of the time, although their responses were often more subtle and harder to read in such a cursory experience.

7. *By which findings will coresearchers feel most accurately represented?* If forced to choose one set of findings, all coresearchers but one felt most completely represented by the artistic analysis. But the group unanimously agreed that the combination of the three was the best approach for fuller understanding.

Overall, I was satisfied with the project and plan to use it again. I will need to give further thought to how to analyze the textual data in a way that engages the students more fully in the task and teaches them more about how textual data analysis is actually done. I also hope to become increasingly comfortable with statistical concepts so that I can make the quantitative analysis as clear and stimulating as the qualitative analysis.

BIBLIOGRAPHY

Adler, J. (1992). Body and soul. *American Journal of Dance Therapy*, 14(2):73-94.

Allen, P. (1995). *Art is a way of knowing*. Boston: Shambhala.

American Dance Therapy Association. (1969). *Code of ethical practice.* Columbia, MD.

American Dance Therapy Association. (1981). *Compendium of presenters' abstracts: Sixteenth Annual Conference: Research as a creative process*. Columbia, MD.

American Dance Therapy Association. (1998). American Dance Therapy Association Homepage. Research. http://www.adta.org.

Avens, R. (1980). *Imagination is reality.* Irving, TX: Spring Publications.

Barone, T. & Eisner, E. (1997). Arts-based educational research. In R. Jaeger (pp. 73 1-N 116). (Ed.). *Complementary methods for research in education.* Washington, DC: American Educational Research Association.

Barry, D. (1996). Artful inquiry: A symbolic constructivist approach to social science research. *Qualitative Inquiry*, 2(4): 411-438.

Barzun, J. (1973). *The use and abuse of art*. Princeton, NJ: Princeton University Press.

Bastick, T. (1982). *Intuition: How we think and act*. New York: Wiley.

Begley, S. (1998 July 20). Science finds god. *Newsweek*, Vol. 132 n. 3, 46-51.

Belenky, M.; Clinchy, B; Goldberger, N., & Tarule, J. (1986). *Womens' ways of knowing*. New York: Basic Books.

Bender, G., & Jones, B. T. (1996). *Still/Here* (adapted for video). Minneapolis: Twin Cities Television.

Beveridge, W.I.B. (1950). *The art of scientific investigation*. New York: Norton.

Blumenfeld-Jones, D. S. (1995). Dance as a mode of research representation. *Qualitative Inquiry*, 1(4): 391-401.

Bohm, D., (1980). *Wholeness and the implicate order*. London: Routledge and Kegan Paul.

Bohm, D. & Peat, D. (1987). *Science, order & creativity*. New York, Bantam.

Brown, R. H. (1977). *A poetic for sociology.* Cambridge, UK: Cambridge University Press.

Bronowski, J. (1981). *The visionary eye*. Cambridge, MA: The MIT Press.

Bruno, C. (1990). Maintaining a concept of the dance in dance/movement-therapy. *American Journal of Dance Therapy*, 12(2): 101-113.

Capra, F. (1982). *The turning point*. New York: Simon & Schuster.

Chaiklin, H. (1968). Research and the development of a profession. In *Proceedings of the Third Annual American Dance Therapy Association Conference - Ed. S. Chaiklin* (pp. 64-74). Columbia, MD: American Dance Therapy Association.

Chaiklin, H. (1997). Research and the development of a profession revisited. *American Journal of Dance Therapy*, 19(2): 93-103.

Clifford, J., & Marcus, G.E. (Eds.).(1986). *Writing culture: the poetics and politics of ethnography.* Berkeley CA: University of California Press.

Collingwood, R.G. (1939). *The principles of art.* London: Oxford University Press.

Croce, A. (1994, December 26). Discussing the undiscussable. *The New Yorker.* 54-60. - v. 70, n. 43.

Csikszentmihalyi, & Robinson., (1990). *The art of seeing.* Malibu, CA: J.P. Getty Press.

Daly, A. (1997). The long days journey of Bill T. Jones. America dancing: The revolution goes world-wide. Washington, DC: *The Kennedy Center 1997-1998 Season Brochure.*

Denzin, N. K., & Lincoln, Y. S. (Eds.). (1994). *Handbook of qualitative research.* Thousand Oaks, CA: Sage.

Denzin, N. K. & Lincoln, Y. S. (1995). Editors' introduction. *Qualitative Inquiry*, 1(1): 3-6.

Dewey, J. (1934/1976). *Art as experience.* In A. Hofstadter & R. Kuhn, (Eds.), *Philosophies of art and beauty.* (pp. 577-646). Chicago: The University of Chicago Press.

Dissanayake, E. (1995). *Homo aestheticus.* Seattle, WA: University of Washington Press.

Diversi, M. (1998). Glimpses of street life: Representing lived experience through short stories. *Qualitative Inquiry*, 4(2): 131-147.

Donmoyer, R., & Yenie-Donmoyer, J. (1995). Data as drama: Reflections of the use of readers theatre as a mode of qualitative data display. *Qualitative Inquiry*, 1(4): 402-428.

Duffy, M. (1995, February 6). Push comes to shove. *Time*, 145: 68-70.

Edinger, E. F. (1990). *The living psyche.* Wilmette, IL: Chiron Publications.

Edwards, D. (1993). Why don't arts therapists do research? In H. Payne (Ed.), *Handbook of inquiry in the arts therapies.* London: Jessica Kingsley Publishers. (pp. 7-15.)

Einstein, A. (1945/1952). Letter to Jacques Hadamar. In B. Ghiselin (Ed.). *The creative process* (p. 43). New York: New American Library.

Eisner, E. (1976). Educational connoisseurship and educational criticism: Their forms and functions is educational evaluation. *Journal of Aesthetic Education, Bicentennial Issue*, 10(3-4):, 135-140.

Eisner, E. (1977). On the uses of educational connoisseurship and educational criticism for evaluating classroom life. *Teachers College Record*, 78(3): 345-358.

Eisner, E. (1981, April). On the differences between scientific and artistic approaches to qualitative inquiry. *Educational Researcher*, Vol. 10 5-9.

Eisner, E. (1985a). *The art of educational evaluation: A personal view.* Philadelphia: Falmer Press.

Eisner, E. (Ed.) (1985b). *Learning and teaching the ways of knowing.* Chicago: The

University of Chicago Press.

Eisner, E. (1985c). Aesthetic modes of knowing. In E. Eisner. (Ed.), *Learning and teaching the ways of knowing*. Chicago: the University of Chicago Press.

Eisner, E. (1991). *The enlightened eye*. New York: Macmillan.

Eisner, E. (1995). What artistically crafted research can help us understand-about schools. *Educational Theory*, 45(1): 1-6.

Eisner, E. (1997). The new frontier in qualitative research methods. *Qualitative Inquiry*, 3(3): 259-273.

Ellis, C., & Bochner, A. (Eds.) (1996). *Composing ethnography*. Walnut Creek,CA: Alta Mira.

Fenner, P. (1996). Heuristic research study: Self-therapy using the brief image-making experience. *The Arts in Psychotherapy*, 23(1): 37-51.

Finley, S., & Knowles, G. (1995). Researcher as artist/artist as researcher. *Qualitative Inquiry*, 1(1): 110-142.

Fisher, A.C. (1992). *Dance/movement therapy abstracts: Doctoral dissertations, master's theses, and special projects through 1990*. Columbia, MD: American Dance Therapy Association.

Fledderjohn, H., & Sewickley, J. (1993). *An annotated bibliography of dance/movement therapy, 1940-1990*. Columbia, MD: American Dance Therapy Association.

Forinash, M. (1993). An exploration into qualitative research in music therapy. *The Arts in Psychotherapy*, 20: 69-73.

Fraleigh, S.H. (1987). *Dance and the lived body*. Pittsburgh, PA:: University of Pittsburgh Press.

Gantt, L. (1986). Systematic investigation of art works. *American Journal of Art Therapy*, 24: 111-118.

Gardner, H. (1985). *Frames of mind*. New York: Basic Books.

Gates, H. L. (1994, November). The body politic. *New Yorker* XX: 112-124. Vol. 30 n. 39.

Geertz, C. (1983). *Local knowledge: Further essays in interpretive anthropology*. New York: Basic Books.

Geertz, C. (1988). *Works and lives: The anthropologist as author*. Stanford, CA: Stanford University Press.

Giorgi, A. (1986). Status of qualitative research in the human sciences; A limited interdisciplinary and international perspective. *Methods*, 1(1): 29-62.

Glesne, C. (1997). That rare feeling: Re-presenting research through poetic transcription. *Qualitative Inquiry*, 3(2): 202-221.

Goellner, E., & Murphy, J.S. (1995). *Bodies of the text: Dance as theory, literature as dance*. New Brunswick, NJ: Rutgers University Press.

Goldwater, R. (1973). Art and anthropology: Some comparisons of methodology. In (Ed.). A. Forge, *Primitive art and society*. London: Oxford University Press.

Greene, T. (1940/1969). Art as an expressive vehicle. In J. Hospers (Ed.), *Introductory readings in aesthetics.*. New York: Free Press.

Griffin, D. R. (1988). *The reenchantment of science*. Albany, NY: The State University of New York.

Guba, E. (1990). *The paradigm dialogue.* Thousand Oaks, CA: Sage.

Guba, E., & Lincoln, Y. (1989). *Fourth generation evaluation.* Newbury Park, CA: Sage.

Harman, W. W. (1996). The shortcomings of Western science. *Qualitative Inquiry,* 2(1): 30-38.

Hawkins, A. (1991). The intuitive process as a force in change. *American Journal of Dance Therapy,* 13(2). 105-116.

Hawkins, P. (1988). A phenomenological psychodrama workshop. In P. Reason, (Ed.). *Human inquiry in action.* (pp. 60 78). Thousand Oaks, CA: Sage.

Heidegger, M. (1971/1976). Poetry, language, thought. In A. Hofstadter & R. Kuhns (Eds.), *Philosophies of art and beauty.* (pp. 647-708). Chicago: The University of Chicago Press.

Hering, D. (1995, April). Bill T. Jones/Arnie Zane Dance Company Review. *Dance Magazine,* Vol. 69:77-78.

Herschel, A. J. (1962). *The prophets.* New York: Harper and Row.

Hofstadter, A., & Kuhns, R. (Eds.). (1976). *Philosophies of art and beauty.* Chicago: The University of Chicago Press.

Holtz, G. (1990). Guest editorial: Suggested research - My top 10! *American Journal of Dance Therapy,* 12(1): 1-7.

Hoshmand, L.T. Tsoi. (1989). Alternative research paradigms: A review and teaching proposal. *The Counseling Psychologist,* 17(1): 3-79.

Jaeger. R. (Ed.). (1997). *Complementary methods for research in education.* Washington, DC: American Educational Research Association.

Janesick, V.J. (1994). The dance of qualitative research design. In N.K. Denzin & Y.S Lincoln (Eds.), *Handbook of qualitative research.* (pp. 209-219). Thousand Oaks, CA: Sage.

Johnson, G. (1998 June, 30-). Science and religion: Bridging the great divide. *The New York Times.* p. C4.

Jones, B. T. (1995). *Last night on earth.* New York: Pantheon Books.

Jones, B. T. (1997). *The Marian Chace Foundation Lecture: A moving dialogue with Bill T. Jones.* Columbia, MD: American Dance Therapy Association.

Junge, M., & Linesch, D. (1993). Our own voices: New paradigms for art theapy research. *The Arts in Psychotherapy,* 20. 61-67.

Knill, P.; Barba, H. N., & Fuchs, B.N. (1995). *Minstrels of soul: Intermodal expressive arts therapies.* Toronto, Canada: Palmerston Press.

Kuhn, T. (1970). *The structure of scientific revolutions.* Chicago, IL: University of Chicago Press.

Landy, R. (1993). Introduction: A research agenda for the creative arts therpies. *Arts in Psychotherapy.* 20: 1-2.

Lawrence-Lightfoot, S., & Davis, J.H. (1997). *The art and science of protraiture.* San Francisco: Jossey-Bass.

Levy, F. J. (1992). *Dance/movement therapy: A healing art.* Reston, VA: National Dance Association.

Marshall, J. (1981). Making sense as a personal process. In P. Reason & J. Rowan (Eds.) *Human inquiry.* New York: Wiley & Sons.

Maykut, P,. & Morehouse, R. (1994). *Beginning qualitative research.* Washington DC: The Falmer Press.

McGettigan, T. (1997). Uncorrected insight: Metaphor and transcendence "after truth" in qualitative inquiry. *Qualitative Inquiry,* 3(3): 366-383.

McNiff, S.(1986).Freedom of research and artistic inquiry. *The Arts in Psychotherapy,* 13(4). 279-284.

McNiff, S. (1987). Research and scholarship in the creative arts therapies. *The Arts in Psychotherapy,* 14(2). 285-292.

McNiff, S. (1992). *Art as medicine.* Boston: Shambhala Books.

McNiff, S. (1993). The authority of experience. *The Arts in Psychotherapy,* 20: 3-9.

McNiff, S. (1998). *Art-based research.* London: Jessica Kingsley.

Meekums, B. (1993). Research as an act of creation. In H. Payne(Ed.), *Handbook of inquiry in the arts therapies* (pp. 130-137). London: Jessica Kingsley.

Meekums, B., & Payne, H. (1993). Emerging methodology in dance movement therapy research. In H. Payne (Ed.), *Handbook of inquiry in the arts therapies* (pp. 164-176). London: Jessica Kingsley.

Mienczakowski, J. (1992). *Syncing out loud: A journey into illness.* Brisbane, Australia: Griffith University Reprographics.

Mienczakowski, J. (1994a). Reading and writing research, National Association of Drama Education. *International Research,* 18(2): 45-54.

Mienczakowski, J. (1994b). Theatrical and theoretical experimentation in ethnography and dramatic form. *ND, Journal of National Drama,* 2(2): 6-23.

Mienczakowski, J. (1995a). Ethnographic theatre: Reading and writing research. *ND, Journal of National Drama,* 3(3): 8-12.

Mienczakowski, J. (1995b). The theater of ethnography: The reconstruction of ethnography into theater with emancipatory potential. *Qualitative Inquiry,* Vol. 1. 3. 360-375.

Mienczakowski, J. (1996). An ethnographic act: The construction of consensual theater. In C. Ellis & A. Bochner (Eds.), *Composing ethnography,* (pp. 244-264). Walnut Creek, CA: Alta Mira.

Mienczakowski, J.; Smith, R., & Sinclair, M. (1996). On the road to catharsis: A theoretical framework for change. *Qualitative Inquiry,* 2(4): 439-462.

Milberg, D. (1977, Fall/Winter). Directions for research in dance/movement therapy. *American Journal of Dance Therapy,* Vol. 1. no. 2:14-17.

Mitroff, I.I., & Kilmann, R.H. (1978). *Methodological approaches to social science.* San Francisco: Jossey-Bass.

Mooney, R.L. (1963). A conceptual model for integrating four approaches to the identification of creative talent. In C.W. Taylor & F. Barron (Eds.), *Scientific creativity: Its recognition and development.* (pp. 331-340). New York: Wiley.

Morgan, D. (1967/1969). Must art tell the truth? In J. Hospers(Ed.), *Introductory readings in aesthetics.* (pp. 225-241). New York: Free Press.

Moustakas, C. (1990). *Heuristic research.* Newbury Park, CA: Sage.

Moyers, B. (1997). *Bill T. Jones: Still/Here with Bill Moyers.* Princeton: Films for the Humanities & Sciences.

Nachmanovitch, S. (1990). *Free play.* New York: G. P. Putnam's Sons.

Nisbet, R. (1976). *Sociology as an art form.* New York: Oxford University Press.

Noddings, N., & Shore, P. (1984). *Awakening the inner eye: Intuition in education.* New York: Teacher's College Press.

Oldfather, P., & West, J. (1994). Qualitative research as jazz. *Educational Researcher,* 23(8): 22-26.

Panek, R. (1999, February 14). Art and science: A universe apart? *The New York Times.* pp. sec. 2. 1,39.

Payne, H. (1993). *Handbook of inquiry in the arts therapies.* London: Jessica Kingsley.

Phillips, D.C. (1995). Art as research, research as art. *Educational Theory.* 45(1): 71-84.

Poincare, H. (1908/1952). Mathematical creation. In Brewster Ghiselin (Ed.), *The creative process* (p. 33). New York: New American Library.

Polanyi, M. (1966). *The tacit dimension.* Garden City, NJ: Doubleday.

Politsky, R. (1995). Toward a typology of research in the creative arts therapies. *Arts in Psychotherapy,* 22(4): 307-314.

Reason, P. (Ed.). (1988). *Human inquiry in action.* Thousand Oaks, CA: Sage.

Reason, P., & Rowan, J. (Eds.) (1981). *Human inquiry.* New York: John Wiley & Sons.

Reason, P., & Hawkins, P. (1988). Storytelling as inquiry. In P. Reason (Ed.), *Human inquiry in action.* (p. 79-101). Thousand Oaks, CA: Sage.

Richardson, L. (1990a). *Writing strategies: Reaching diverse audiences.* Thousand Oaks, CA: Sage.

Richardson, L. (1990b). Narrative and sociology. *Journal of Contemporary Ethnography,* 19(1): 116-135.

Richardson, L. (1991). Postmodern social theory: Representational practices. *Sociological Theory,* 9: 173-180.

Richardson, L. (1992). The consequences of poetic representation; Writing the other, rewriting the self. In C. Ellis & M.G. Flaherty (Eds.), *Investigating subjectivity: Research on lived experience.* (pp. 125-140) Thousand Oaks, CA: Sage.

Richardson, L. (1993). Poetics, dramatics, and transgressive validity: The case of the skipped line. *Sociological Quarterly,* 34(4): 695-710.

Richardson, L. (1994). Writing: A method of inquiry. In N. Denzin & Y. S. Lincoln (Eds.), *Handbook of qualitative research.* Thousand Oaks, CA: Sage.

Richardson, L. (1995). Writing stories: Co-authoring "The Sea Monster," a writing story. *Qualitative Inquiry,* 1(2): 189-203.

Richardson, L. (1997). *Fields of play: Constructing an academic life.* New Brunswick, NJ: Rutgers University Press.

Ritter, M. ,& Low, K. G. (1996). The effectiveness of dance/movement therapy. *The Arts in Psychotherapy,* (pp. 296-305) 23(3): 249-260.

Rogers, C. (1976). Toward a Theory of creativity. In A. Rothenberg & C. R. Hausman (Eds.), *The creativity question.* Durham, NC: Duke University Press.

Rubik, B. (1996). *Life at the edge of science.* Philadelphia: The Institute of Frontier Science.

Sandelowski, M. (1994) The proof is in the pottery: Toward a poetic for qualitative inquiry. In J. Morse (Ed.), *Critical issues in qualitative research methods,* (pp. 46-63). Thousand Oaks, CA: Sage.

Schaffer, S. (1994). Making up discovery. In M. Boden (Ed.), *Dimensions of creativity*, (pp. 13-51). Cambridge, MA: MIT Press.

Serlin, I. (1993). Root images of healing in dance therapy. *American Journal of Dance Therapy*, 15(2): 65-76.

Shallcross, D. J., & Sisk, D.A. (1989). *Intuition: An inner way of knowing*. Buffalo, NY: Bearly Limited.

Shapiro, L. (1995, February 6). The art of victimization. *Newseek*, 125,63.

Sheridan, A. (1980). *Michel Foucault: The will to truth*. London: Tavistock.

Siegel, M. B. (1996). Virtual criticism and the dance of death. *The Drama Review* ,40(2): 60-70.

Sims, C. (1996, February). Jones: Race a factor in Croce's New Yorker "Victim Art" article. *Dance Magazine*, Vol. 70, n. z.: 34.

Sorrell, W. (1971). *The dancer's image*. New York: Columbia University Press.

Steiner, W. (1995). *The scandal of pleasure*. Chicago: The University of Chicago Press.

Stinson, S. (1995). Body of knowledge. *Educational Theory*, 45(1): 43-54.

Strauss, A., & Corbin, J. (1990). *Basics of qualitative research: Grounded theory procedures and techniques*. Thousand Oaks, CA: Sage.

Talbot, M. (1991). *The holographic universe*. New York: Harper Perennial.

Taylor, J. (1998). *Poetic knowledge*. Albany, NY: State University of New York Press.

Teachout, T. (1995, March). Victim art. *Commentary*, 99,3: 58-61.

Temin, C. (1997, January 17). Moyers dives into Jones' craft. *Boston Globe*, p. D18.

Tesch, R. (1990). *Qualitative research: Analysis types and software tools*. New York: Falmer Press.

Torossian, A. (1937). *A guide to aesthetics*. Stanford, CA: Stanford University Press.

Weissman, D. (1993). *Truth's debt to value*. New Haven, CT: Yale University Press.

Wilber, K. (1981). Reflections of the New Age paradigm: An interview with Ken Wilber. *ReVision*, 4(1): 53-74.

Yablonsky, L. (1995, March). Ensemble work. *Art in America*, 83,3: 55-56.

Ziller, R. (1990). *Photographing the self*. Newbury Park, CA: Sage.

INDEX

153

Charles C Thomas
P U B L I S H E R • L T D.

Leader In Creative Therapies Publications

► denotes new publication

► Esping, Amber—**SYMPATHETIC VIBRATIONS: A Guide for Private Music Teachers.** '00, 158 pp. (8 1/2 x 11), 10 il.

► Peters, Jacqueline Schmidt—**MUSIC THERAPY: AN INTRODUCTION. (2nd Ed.)** '00, 386 pp. (8 1/2 x 11), 2 tables.

► Johnson, David Read—**ESSAYS ON THE CREATIVE ARTS THERAPIES: Imaging the Birth of a Profession.** '99, 228 pp. (7 x 10), 14 il., 12 tables, $43.95, cloth, $29.95, paper.

► Williams, Yvonne B.—**THE ART OF DYING: A Jungian View of Patients' Drawings.** '99, 242 pp. (6 3/4 x 9 3/4), 31 il. (26 in color), $29.95, cloth.

Frostig, Karen & Michele Essex—**EXPRESSIVE ARTS THERAPIES IN SCHOOLS: A Super-vision and Program Development Guide.** '98, 128 pp. (8 1/2 x 11), 8 il., $20.95, spiral (paper).

Moon, Bruce L.—**THE DYNAMICS OF ART AS THERAPY WITH ADOLESCENTS.** '98, 260 pp. (7 x 10), 27 il., $52.95, cloth, $ 39.95, paper.

Benenzon, Rolando O.—**MUSIC THERAPY THEORY AND MANUAL: Contributions to the Knowledge of Nonverbal Contexts. (2nd Ed.)** '97, 296 pp. (7 x 10), 44 il., $59.95, cloth, $44.95, paper.

Spencer, Linda Bushell—**HEAL ABUSE AND TRAUMA THROUGH ART: Increasing Self-Worth, Healing of Initial Wounds, and Creating a Sense of Connectivity.** '97, 250 pp. (7 x 10), 10 il., $59.95, cloth, $39.95, paper.

Moon, Bruce L.—**ART AND SOUL: Reflections on an Artistic Psychology.** '96, 156 pp. (7 x l0), 15 il., $36.95, cloth, $25.95, paper.

Moon, Bruce L.—**EXISTENTIAL ART THERAPY: The Canvas Mirror. (2nd Ed.)** '95, 230 pp. (7 x 10), 21 il,$52.95, cloth, $35.95, paper.

Horovitz-Darby, Ellen G.—**SPIRITUAL ART THERAPY: An Alternate Path.** '94, 186 pp. (7 x 10), 33 il., $44.95, cloth, $31.95, paper.

Singer, Florence—**STRUCTURING CHILD BEHAVIOR THROUGH VISUAL ART: A Therapeutic, Individualized Art Program to Develop Positive Behavior Attitudes in Children.** '80, 144 pp., 33 il., $27.95, cloth, $16.95, paper.

► St. John, Iris—**CREATIVE SPIRITUALITY FOR WOMEN: Developing a Positive Sense of Self Through Spiritual Growth Exercises.** '00, 168 pp. (8 1/2 x 11) , 1 table, $26.95, spiral (paper).

► Horovitz, Ellen G.—**A LEAP OF FAITH: The Call to Art.** '99, 210 pp. (7 x 10), 66 il., (4 in color), $44.95, cloth, $31.95, paper.

► Lantz, Jim—**MEANING-CENTERED MARITAL AND FAMILY THERAPY: Learning to Bear the Beams of Love.** '00, 166 pp. (7 x 10), 12 il., $36.95, cloth, $23.95, paper.

Feder, Bernard & Elaine Feder—**THE ART AND SCIENCE OF EVALUATION IN THE ARTS THERAPIES: How Do You Know What's Working?** '98, 398 pp. (7 x 10), 25 il., $75.95, cloth, $59.95, paper.

Makin, Susan R.—**POETIC WISDOM: Revealing and Healing.** '98, 246 pp. (7 x 10), $50.95, cloth, $37.95 paper.

Brooke, Stephanie L.—**ART THERAPY WITH SEXUAL ABUSE SURVIVORS.** '97, 188 pp. (7 x 10), 31 il., $42.95, cloth, $26.95, paper.

Bush, Janet—**THE HANDBOOK OF SCHOOL ART THERAPY: Introducing Art Therapy Into a School System.** '97, 206 pp. (7 x 10), 26 il., $48.95, cloth, $35.95, paper.

Brooke, Stephanie L.—**A THERAPIST'S GUIDE TO ART THERAPY ASSESSMENTS: Tools of the Trade.** '96, 164 pp. (7 x 10), 7 il., $34.95, cloth, $24.95, paper.

Plach, Tom—**THE CREATIVE USE OF MUSIC IN GROUP THERAPY. (2nd Ed.)** '96, 84 pp. (7 x 10), $31.95, cloth, $20.95 paper.

Makin, Susan R—**A CONSUMER'S GUIDE TO ART THERAPY—For Prospective Employers, Clients and Students.** '94, 112 pp. (7 x 10), $31.95, cloth, $18.95, paper.

Exiner, Johanna & Denis Kelynack—**DANCE THERAPY REDEFINED: A Body Approach to Therapeutic Dance.** '94, 130 pp. (7 x 10), 12 il. $32.95.

Levick, Myra F.—**THEY COULD NOT TALK AND SO THEY DREW: Children's Styles of Coping and Thinking.** '83, 240 pp. 134 il., 11 tables, $56.95, cloth, $40.95, paper.

Books sent on approval • Shipping charges: $5.50 U.S. / $6.50 Canada • Prices subject to change without notice

Contact us to order books or a free catalog with over 800 titles

Call 1-800-258-8980 or 1-217-789-8980 or Fax 1-217-789-9130
2600 South First Street • Springfield • Illinois • 62704
Complete catalog available at www.ccthomas.com • books@ccthomas.com